COOKIE CLUB

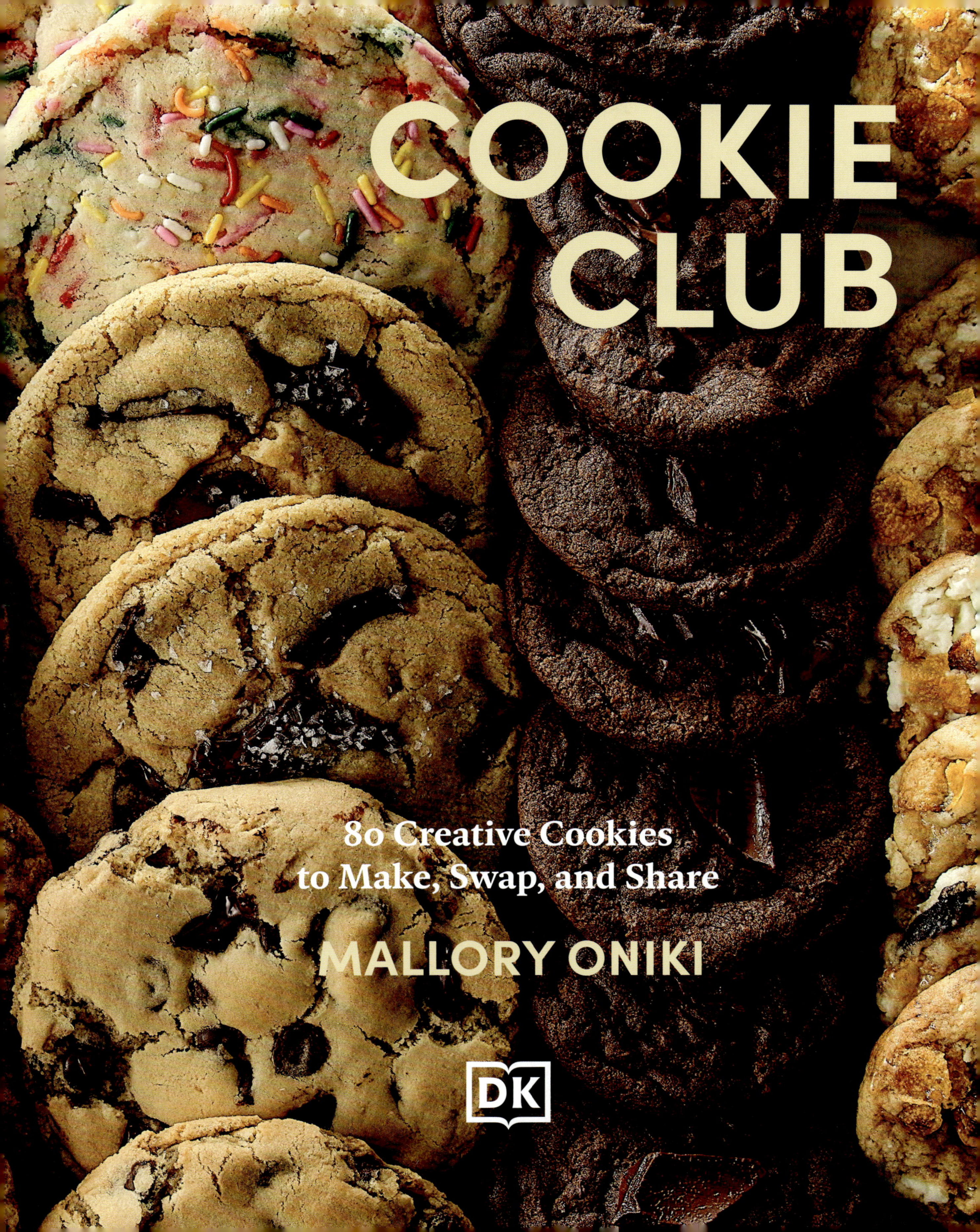
COOKIE CLUB
80 Creative Cookies to Make, Swap, and Share
MALLORY ONIKI
DK

Publisher Mike Sanders
Art & Design Director William Thomas
Editorial Director Ann Barton
Executive Editor Olivia Peluso
Editorial Assistant Resham Anand
Photographer Nico Schinco
Food Stylist Kaitlin Wayne
Prop Stylists Maeve Sheridan & Ashleigh Sarbone
Illustrator Giovana Cavalcante
Recipe Testers Ben Weiner & Gregory Weinstein
Recipe Editor Taylor Plett
Copyeditor West Matuszak
Proofreaders Bianca Bosman & Georgette Beatty
Indexer Beverlee Day

First American Edition, 2026
Published in the United States by DK Publishing
1745 Broadway, 20th Floor, New York, NY 10019

The authorized representative in the EEA is
Dorling Kindersley Verlag GmbH. Arnulfstr. 124, 80636 Munich, Germany

26 27 28 29 30 13 12 11 10 9 8 7 6 5 4
003–348425–Apr/2026

A catalog record for this book
is available from the Library of Congress.
ISBN 978-0-5939-6515-3

DK books are available at special discounts when purchased
in bulk for sales promotions, premiums, fund-raising, or educational use.
For details, contact SpecialSales@dk.com

Printed and bound in Canada

www.dk.com

This book was made with Forest Stewardship Council™ certified paper – one small step in DK's commitment to a sustainable future.
Learn more at
www.dk.com/uk/information/sustainability

To Connor and Emi, my whole world.

CONTENTS

INTRODUCTION

Welcome to the Cookie Club! The only requirement for membership in this club is to love cookies, and if you're reading this book, I assume that includes you! I'm so glad you're here, and I can't wait for you to dive into my world of cookies.

I was nine years old when I baked cookies *all by myself* for the first time. I had baked lots of cookies previously with plenty of help from my mom, but this was the first time I took charge, with no one else overseeing. I must have let the power go to my head, because I unknowingly swapped baking soda for baking powder *and* used a tablespoon instead of a teaspoon. The cookies were a disaster, and my confidence was crushed. But after my devastation wore off, I was determined to make the best cookies in the world.

I didn't start developing my own recipes until I was well into college. I was a poor, starving student who still wanted to eat really well, so I had to get creative. It started with savory foods—I'd look in my fridge and evaluate what ingredients I had on hand and then I'd see what I could come up with. There were a lot of "I'll never be making this again" dishes, but as my skills and confidence grew, those became rarer. Then, slowly, my itch for recipe development bled into baked goods. Baking is much more precise than cooking, and at first, I had no idea what I was doing. But with each recipe, I kept improving. One of the first cookie recipes I ever developed, which became the first cookie recipe I posted on my website, was a carrot cake cookie stuffed with cream cheese frosting (this recipe also made its way into this book, on page 142). It's a miracle those cookies turned out as well as they did because I really didn't know what I was doing, but the recipe is still one of my favorites to this day.

Back then, my website was little more than a dream. I had a very bare-bones site, but I was finishing undergrad and didn't have time to post more than a few times a year. Then, during my last semester, the pandemic hit, and I suddenly had a lot of time on my hands. I decided to start sharing more recipes and actively posting on Instagram and TikTok. My social media growth was small but steady until late 2020, when I started a series called "Cookies Inspired by TV Shows and Movies." Think peanut butter Oreos for *The Parent Trap* (page 180) and coffee cake cookies for *Gilmore Girls* (page 175). The series went absolutely viral and put me on the map, enough to allow me to dive into recipe development and content creation full time at the beginning of 2021.

Though that cookie series ended later that year (but it starts up again on page 173!), cookies continued to be an important part of my content. I now have over 100 cookie recipes on my website, and there are 80 in this book! I often am asked if I ever get sick of cookies, and I truly don't. I've just always felt so drawn to cookies. They're the goodie that everyone likes. The dessert you gather to make together or eat together. The treat you bring when someone has just had a baby or experienced a breakup. When I had my daughter, Emi, cookies became an outlet for me to express myself—a way for me to define my identity outside of just being a mom (and I love being a mom with my whole heart). And now she gets to say that her mom makes cookies for a living. How cool is that?

I know cookies are just butter, sugar, and flour, but they're more than that for me, and I hope you feel that way, too. I hope the recipes in this book are an outlet for you, a reason to gather, an excuse to knock on your neighbor's door. And I hope this feels like so much more than a standard baking book. I want it to be a place where you can find flavors you already know and love, where you also get the confidence to explore combinations you've never tried before. So as president of the Cookie Club, welcome. I hope you stay a while and eat a few cookies while you're here.

HOW TO USE THIS BOOK

PLEASE READ BEFORE BAKING

These are all the things you need to know to make all the recipes in this book.

- **Read the recipe all the way through before baking.** There's nothing like craving a fresh, gooey cookie and then realizing the dough needs to be chilled overnight. Save yourself and read the entire recipe before diving in!
- **Always try the dough (and don't tell anyone I said that!).** Tasting a little bit of the dough will help you know if you accidentally left out an ingredient. No salt? You'll know.
- **Read your labels.** The first time I ever baked cookies by myself, I switched the baking soda and baking powder, and it led to a disaster. Make sure you are reading the labels and adding the right things to the dough.
- **Scrape down the sides of the bowl!** All the time! Any time you add a new ingredient and mix, scrape the bowl before adding another one. This ensures you don't have any weird pockets in the dough.
- **Don't overmix the dough.** No one likes a tough cookie. When you add your flour, mix *just* until the flour is combined. If you mix too much, too much gluten will develop in your dough, which creates a bad cookie.
- **Use this book.** If there aren't chocolate smudges on at least five pages of this book, I'll be a little upset. OK, if you like things clean, that's fine, too. But make these recipes your own! If you don't like raisins but want to make the Oatmeal Raisin Cookies (page 83), use dried cranberries or chocolate chips. Just don't change anything structural to the cookies (the amount of leaveners and sugar); they won't turn out well.
- **If you don't want huge cookies, that's fine.** Most of my cookies are big. I like huge cookies. I'm not always eating an entire cookie in one sitting, but I'm usually guilty of taking small slices of the cookie until it's 90 percent gone. But if you like smaller cookies, most of these recipes can be made smaller! Use a smaller cookie scoop and decrease the baking time by 2 or 3 minutes depending on their size. Just watch for the same visual cues and you should be good to go.

WHAT TO DO WITH LEFTOVER COOKIES

You may have a few spare cookies and want to keep them for later. Store any extra cookies in an airtight container at room temperature for up to 5 days (unless the recipe directs you to store them in the fridge). To freeze the dough and bake later, scoop the dough onto a baking sheet or plate lined with parchment paper. Chill the dough in the fridge for 1 hour and then transfer the dough balls to an airtight container for up to 3 months. Bake straight from the freezer and add 2 or 3 minutes of bake time. For any cookies with frosting or a topping (excluding streusel), freeze without the topping, then add after baking. To freeze baked cookies, place the cookies in an airtight container and transfer to the freezer. Let the cookies thaw at room temperature and then enjoy.

EQUIPMENT

Here are the essentials for making sure your cookies turn out perfectly each time.

- **Stand mixer or hand mixer:** It's convenient to have both, but you can bake your way through this entire book with one or the other. I strongly prefer a stand mixer, but if you only have a hand mixer, you'll be just fine. I love my KitchenAid 5 Quart Tilt-Head Stand Mixer. It's plenty large for these recipes, even big enough to double them. The flat beater and wire whip are the only attachments you'll need.
- **Baking sheets:** Can't bake cookies without these! Two standard half-sheet (13 × 18-inch/33 × 45 cm) pans are recommended for each recipe. You can get away with one, but you'll just have to bake the first half of the cookies, wait for the pan to cool off, and then bake the rest. Make sure your baking sheets are light in color; dark baking sheets will get too hot in the oven and will cause the cookies to get too dark on the bottom.
- **Digital scale: Oh, the age-old debate:** Should you measure ingredients with a digital scale or measuring cups? In the US, most of us learn to use solely measuring cups (I know I did), but for baking, a digital scale just makes sense. It is *far* more accurate (see page 41 for more information) and uses fewer dishes! Throw your stand mixer bowl on the scale and drop the ingredients straight in. It makes everything much simpler and more accurate. Home cooks deserve more, and buying yourself a digital scale is a great place to start.
- **Measuring cups:** For those of you who refuse to buy a digital scale, I've provided measurements in cups as well. Just make sure you are measuring each ingredient correctly (see page 41 for information on how to correctly measure flour with a measuring cup).
- **Measuring spoons:** Gram measurements are provided for all measurements ¼ cup and above, so for anything less than that, you'll need your handy-dandy measuring spoons!
- **Rubber spatula:** Always have one of these handy! You'll need it to scrape the bowl between each addition of ingredients so you get perfectly mixed dough.
- **Small, medium, and large mixing bowls:** You'll need a large mixing bowl to make any cookie dough. When using my stand mixer, I use the large bowl that attaches to it to streamline everything. You'll need medium and small bowls to mix up anything else or portion out ingredients.
- **Oven thermometer:** Ovens are so unpredictable! Whenever I move to a new place, I have to spend a few months "dating" my oven to see how it reacts. Does it heat up quickly? Does it accurately hold its temperature? Are there hot spots? For my current oven, I've found it takes about 10 minutes longer to *actually* heat up than when it first beeps to indicate that it's up to temp. So, if you haven't spent some time dating your oven yet, here's your push to do so. Buying an oven thermometer will help significantly. I leave mine in my oven at all times.

- **Cutting board and chef's knife:** These cookies have lots of toppings and mix-ins! For several cookie recipes, you'll need a cutting board and chef's knife to chop these ingredients.
- **Metal spatula:** There's nothing worse than having a thick spatula catch the edge of a freshly baked cookie and ruin your perfect creation. A thin, sturdy metal spatula will help you seamlessly transfer your warm cookies from the baking sheet to the cooling rack, without any cookie fatalities.
- **Cooling rack:** Occasionally cookies don't even make it to the cooling rack because I can't help but dive in early, but if you can wait, a cooling rack is so helpful. It allows heat to escape from all sides of your cookies so they cool evenly and don't overcook.
- **Cookie scoop:** I cannot live without my cookie scoops! This book is filled with scoop-and-drop cookies, so a cookie scoop will be your best friend. It speeds the process up and creates uniformly sized cookies. I suggest buying a three-pack, which includes large (4-tablespoon/2-ounce), medium (2-tablespoon/1-ounce), and small (1-tablespoon/½-ounce) scoops.

Then, there's your "nice to haves," the things that are optional but will bring your cookies to the next level.

- **Piping bags and tips:** A handful of cookies include frosting or some other topping. For several of them, piping the topping makes the cookie much prettier. Piping bags definitely aren't necessary, though, and a plastic sandwich bag with the corner cut off can always do the trick, too.
- **Rolling pin:** A few cookies in this book need to be rolled out. A rolling pin is great, but a wine bottle or jar of pasta sauce can be used in a pinch!
- **Kitchen torch:** There are two cookies where a kitchen torch really comes in handy: the Lemon Meringue Cookies on page 146 (to toast meringue) and the Crème Brûlée Cookies on page 154 (to melt sugar). A kitchen torch is the easiest and safest way to go, but if you don't have one, you can use the broiler in your oven instead (but please be careful to not burn anything, cookies included!).
- **Microplane:** Lemon and lime zest make their way into a few cookies in this book, and a microplane is helpful here. If you don't have one, the small side of a box grater can work as well.

INGREDIENTS

We'll get more into the weeds of most of these ingredients in the Cookie Science chapter (page 33), but here are the basic ingredients you'll need to make almost any cookie in this book.

- **Butter:** I prefer salted butter (more on that hot debate on page 35), but unsalted will work fine if that's all you have on hand.
- **Granulated sugar:** The fine, uniform crystals of refined white sugar dissolve easily and provide cookies with not only sweetness but structure and texture as well.
- **Brown sugar (dark and light):** You can use either in your recipes, but I usually prefer dark brown sugar, which has more molasses and therefore more depth of flavor.
- **Powdered sugar:** Granulated sugar is blended into a fine powder to make powdered sugar. It's mostly used in frosting, occasionally in the cookie dough.
- **Eggs:** For the most consistent results, use large eggs for any recipe in this book.
- **Vanilla extract:** I *love* vanilla extract. It has a rich, warm, slightly sweet flavor that adds such a depth to a cookie. If it's in your budget, vanilla bean paste has an even more potent flavor.
- **Flour:** Though all-purpose flour is by far the most frequently used flour in my cookies, if you make every single recipe in this book, you'll need the following six flours: all-purpose flour, almond flour, bread flour, whole wheat flour, rye flour, and masa harina.
- **Cornstarch:** Cornstarch is a powder made from corn kernels that is commonly used as a thickening agent in cooking and baking. I use it occasionally in my cookie recipes to prevent cookies from spreading too much when they bake. It also aids in creating a tender cookie that stays soft for several days.
- **Oats:** I love oats in a cookie. They add such a nice chew and keep cookies soft. For all the recipes in this book that call for oats, I always use old-fashioned oats.
- **Baking soda:** This leavener reacts with acidic ingredients (like brown sugar, yogurt, or lemon juice) to help baked goods rise.
- **Baking powder:** This is also a leavener, but unlike baking soda, it doesn't need an external acidic ingredient to activate. It will activate first with moisture and then with heat.
- **Salt:** Salt is beyond essential! I always use Diamond Crystal Kosher Salt for baking. It has the best texture and taste. If you're not using Diamond Crystal Kosher Salt, you'll need to half the salt amount in each recipe by half. For more explanation, see page 44.
- **Spices:** A lot of my recipes call for cinnamon, and a few call for more unique spices like cardamom and cayenne pepper (yep, you read that right!).
- **Chocolate:** It wouldn't be a cookie book without chocolate in all of its forms—chips, bars, white, dark, and more!
- **Cream cheese:** Usually used in frosting and occasionally in the dough itself, cream cheese provides a tangy kick and a smooth texture. Just make sure you are using full-fat cream cheese.

- **Cocoa powder:** Made from roasted and ground cacao beans, cocoa powder will bring out depth in any chocolate cookie.
- **Olive oil:** A couple cookies in this book have olive oil in them instead of butter. This gives the cookies a tender crumb and a tangy, slight olive taste.
- **Tahini:** You'll quickly realize how much I love tahini. It's a paste made from sesame seeds (think peanut butter but made with sesame seeds instead of peanuts). It's creamy and nutty and yields a delightful cookie.
- **Peanut butter:** If you make all the peanut butter cookies in this book, you'll need both natural peanut butter and conventional peanut butter (which has added sugar and stabilizers).

CLUB RULES

In this book, you'll find more than just cookie recipes. If you're holding it in your hands, you now belong to the Cookie Club! I am so honored you are joining us and hope you enjoy every second we spend together. But before we dive into baking, we need to set a few club rules.

Eat cookies and feelings: This is a no-judgment zone. Everything is welcome in this club. Cookies are the ultimate treat for celebration or sadness, drama or triumph. Bring all the feelings and dive into the cookies!

Secrets stay in the mixing bowl: Anything discussed while baking and eating cookies stays in the Cookie Club!

Flour on your shirt = 1 gold star: We embrace the mess. Don't go overboard, but don't stress about flour on your clothes or spilled milk. Crumbs are a sign of a good time!

Baking time is sacred time: When the cookies bake, we give each other our full attention. No phones, zero distractions, just advice, drama, and stories.

Come hungry: *Duh.* Never show up with a full stomach. And if you do, find a way to make more room! These cookies aren't going to eat themselves.

Once a cookie clubber, always a cookie clubber: No matter where you are or where you go, you'll always have a seat at this cookie-filled table.

HOW TO THROW A COOKIE PARTY

In the Cookie Club, we love to throw cookie parties. Here's my guide for how to host your own.

HOW TO PREPARE

- **Choose a theme:** Not only does everyone love a theme, but it also makes it a lot easier for you to plan everything: menu, decorations, guest list, and dress code.
- **Make the dough ahead of time:** Almost all the cookies in this book can be completely or partially made in advance! Cookie dough is quite forgiving and can spend some time in the fridge, so make the dough for each cookie a day or two before your party.
- **Organize your serving dishes:** I like to lay out all the serving dishes I'm going to use and label them with the names of the cookies I'll place on them. This helps you check that all the servingware is clean and everything has a place to go.
- **Prepare to-go containers:** If you want guests to take any cookies home, prepare boxes or bags with ribbons or tags for packing up extra cookies once the party is over.

DAY OF

- **Bake the dough:** All the dough will be prepped, so all you have to do is bake it off. Make sure you do it well before your party starts if the cookies need to be cooled or decorated.
- **Decorate the cookies:** If any of the cookies have a frosting or topping, prepare it on the day of the party (unless a recipe specifically calls for chill time). Get all the cookies decorated and finished before guests arrive (unless you plan to make cookie decorating a part of the party!).
- **Set the mood:** It all depends on what your chosen theme is, but I think every party needs these three mood setters:
  - **Put on a playlist!** Every party needs music, so throw on some tunes that match the vibe.
  - **Set up any decorations or props that match your theme.**
  - **Make sure your home smells good!** It likely already will from all the baking you're doing, but if it needs an extra boost, light a candle or put a simmer pot on the stove.

HOSTING TIPS

- **Label everything:** Clearly label what each cookie is and always include any potential allergies that someone may need to avoid (like dairy or nuts).
- **Offer drinks and savory snacks:** These extras will break up the sweetness of the cookies. Even just a simple bowl of butter popcorn is enough to give people a break from all the sugar, but add as many savory snacks as you'd like. For drinks, match the vibe! Maybe you put out five different types of milk, maybe you include a coffee setup, or maybe you serve a few cocktails. Cookies always need some kind of drink to wash them down.
- **Take pics:** Snap a few pictures of the cookie spread and your guests so you'll have memories that will last long after your guests have gone home. Cookie Club is forever!
- **Include some type of game:** It can be as simple or elaborate as you'd like, but a game is always a great icebreaker and a fun way to get people talking (blind taste tests are always my fave!).

THEMED COOKIE PARTIES

Every good party has a theme, and cookie parties are no exception. Here are my favorite themes for all your cookie party needs!

SPICE IT UP

Host a party serving only spicy foods. Pair these three cookies with your favorite spicy snacks and drinks for a spicy night. Maybe set out a few glasses of milk for those who can't take the heat!

- Spicy CCC (page 71)
- Chili Crisp Cookies (page 106)
- Hot Honey Cookies (page 118)

HOLIDAY PARTY

Everyone wants cookies during the holiday season! Throw up some festive decor, put a cozy simmer pot on the stove, and make sure to provide boxes for people to take home any extra cookies to snack on all season long.

- Soft Gingerbread Cookies (page 87)
- Cinnamon Roll Snickerdoodle Cookies (page 135)
- Shortbread (page 97)
- Raspberry Cheesecake Cookies (page 148)
- Sticky Toffee Pudding Cookies (page 170)
- Stuffed Red Velvet Cookies (page 240)

CHOCOLATE CHIP: HAVE IT YOUR WAY

Host a party all about CCC, and everyone will be happy! You can even turn it into a blind taste test to determine, once and for all, which CCC is actually the best. If you want to go all out, you can make all eleven cookies from the CCC chapter (page 51), or if you want to narrow it down for a taste test, I'd go with these:

- Thin and Crispy CCC (page 56)
- Crunchy Edge, Soft Middle CCC (page 52)
- Thick and Gooey CCC (page 55)
- Brown Butter CCC (page 60)
- Olive Oil CCC (page 63)

BROWN BUTTER EVERYTHING

There are few things I love more than brown butter—I did start a holiday dedicated to it (National Brown Butter Day on September 22), after all—so this is my ideal party. Serve these brown butter cookies, paired with savory snacks for the ultimate brown butter night.

- Brown Butter CCC (page 60)
- Cinnamon and Milk Chocolate Cookies with Hazelnut Cream Filling (page 224)
- Raspberry White Chocolate Cookies (page 243)
- Rice Krispies Treat Cookies (page 162)

SUMMER IS HERE!

Every year when summer rolls around, my life begins again, which is always something to celebrate! These cookies' bright, fresh flavors scream summer.

- Sweet Corn and Blueberry Cookies (page 129)
- Key Lime Pie Cookies (page 123)
- Lemon Tart Cookies (page 167)
- Chilled Peach Pie Cookies (page 132)
- Lemon Cookie Sandwiches with Lemon Curd and Mascarpone Frosting (page 238)
- Strawberry Cheesecake Cookies (page 226)

STAR SIGN PARTY

This party is ideal for any group of friends who love astrology and baking (and who doesn't?). It's the best combination of horoscopes, personality deep dives, and yummy cookies. All the cookies uniquely fit each of the twelve zodiac signs, so there is truly something for everyone. This party is fun at any time of year, but especially at the start of the zodiac calendar (hello, Aries!) in late March or as a New Year's gathering to reflect on the year ahead. Have each guest bring the cookie that correlates with their star sign, or bake them all yourself for the full-year spread!

- **Aries (March 21 to April 19):** Spicy CCC (page 71). Aries are known for their boldness and leadership qualities. They're energetic and competitive, so they need a cookie that can keep up! The Spicy CCC leads with strong CCC flavor, but the kick of the cayenne pepper takes over and packs a punch to your taste buds.
- **Taurus (April 20 to May 20):** Tahini CCC (page 68). Taurus are grounded and loyal. They love comfort, beauty, and the finer things in life. Tahini CCC are rich and indulgent by nature, with pools of chocolate throughout, but are grounded with the nutty, earthy flavor of tahini.
- **Gemini (May 21 to June 20):** Date, Cheddar, and Dark Chocolate Cookies (page 117). Geminis are witty and curious. They are social butterflies who can charm anyone but are also dual-natured and unpredictable. Date, cheddar, and dark chocolate cookies are their twin, with an unpredictable combination of flavors that work beautifully together and unexpectedly please everyone.

- **Cancer (June 21 to July 22):** PB&J Cookie Sandwiches (page 230). Cancers are deeply emotional and nurturing. They tend to romanticize memories and have a strong connection to their roots and childhood. PB&J cookie sandwiches are as comforting and nostalgic as it gets.
- **Leo (July 23 to August 22):** Lemon Meringue Cookies (page 146). Leos are confident and love to shine. They are charismatic and were born to be in the spotlight. Lemon meringue cookies are bold, extra, and unforgettable. They demand your attention, especially when you crack out a kitchen torch to toast the meringue on top.
- **Virgo (August 23 to September 22):** Almond Croissant Cookies (page 158). Virgos are practical and analytical. They are poised, refined, detail-oriented perfectionists. Almond croissant cookies are the only right match for them. These cookies have a sophisticated flavor and presentation, and the dusting of powdered sugar on top is the perfect finishing touch.
- **Libra (September 23 to October 22):** Lemon Cookie Sandwiches with Lemon Curd and Mascarpone Frosting (page 238). Libras are charming and elegant. They are obsessed with balance and love beauty and harmony. These lemon sugar cookie sandwiches are pretty and poised. Soft lemon cookies are sandwiched with a smooth mascarpone frosting filling for a balanced, aesthetic cookie.
- **Scorpio (October 23 to November 21):** Chili Crisp Cookies (page 106). Scorpios are mysterious and intense. They are deeply passionate people who are often very private; there are layers to what they'll let people see. By their name alone, chili crisp cookies are

also mysterious and intense. There are several layers to this cookie: a chili crisp brittle that is spicy, garlicky, sweet, and crunchy, combined with caramelized white chocolate, coconut flakes, and sesame seeds. You'll want nothing more than to explore what lies beneath the surface of this cookie.

- **Sagittarius (November 22 to December 21):** Blood Orange, Cardamom, and Pistachio Cookies (page 114). Sagittarius are adventurous, always chasing the next thrill. They're daring and bright and always down to try something new. These olive oil cookies with blood oranges are bright and unique. An olive oil dough is mixed with cardamom, pistachios, and blood orange zest and then each cookie is dipped in a glowing blood orange icing. It's a combination of flavors you've never tried and one that Sagittarius would be thrilled to.
- **Capricorn (December 22 to January 19):** Brown Butter CCC (page 60). Capricorns are ambitious and goal driven. They're disciplined and sophisticated, and they hold themselves to a high standard. There is no better cookie for Capricorns than brown butter CCC. This sophisticated cookie has no thrills, just flawless execution.
- **Aquarius (January 20 to February 18):** Mango Sticky Rice Cookies (page 156). Aquarius are innovative and quirky. They are one-of-a-kind visionaries who march to the beat of their own drum. These mango sticky rice cookies are as one-of-a-kind as it gets. Coconut-flavored dough is mixed with sticky rice to make a soft, chewy, innovative, and quirky cookie. Each cookie is topped with a smooth whipped cream, fresh mango, and sesame seeds.

- **Pisces (February 19 to March 20):** Sweet Corn and Blueberry Cookies (page 123). Pisces are empathetic, dreamy, and artistic. They are deeply intuitive and compassionate. These sweet corn and blueberry cookies are also imaginative and creative: Corn-studded cookies are dipped in a bright blueberry icing to make a whimsical, artistic treat.

COZY FALL PARTY

Fall is often deemed pumpkin spice latte (PSL) season, but it has so much more to offer. Host a fall-themed cookie party to explore all the warm and comforting flavors of the season. Pair the cookies with PSLs (OK, I gave in) or hot cider to complete the cozy vibe.

- Apple Crisp Cookies (page 152)
- Cinnamon Roll Snickerdoodle Cookies (page 135)
- Stuffed Pumpkin Snickerdoodles (page 234)
- Almond Croissant Cookies (page 158)

GIRLS' NIGHT IN

A GNI cookie party is the perfect way to reconnect, slow down, and indulge in sweets. This cozy, low-pressure party gives you a chance to catch up, laugh, and gossip (let's be real) while you enjoy some cookies. You can bake and decorate the cookies together or have them all prepared beforehand to enjoy while you watch a TV show or movie (maybe *Gilmore Girls* or *Clueless*?)!

- Edible CCC Dough (page 72)
- Swirled Malted Cookies (page 110)
- Banana Pudding Cookies (page 140)
- *Gilmore Girls* Coffee Cake Cookies (page 175)
- *Clueless* Checkerboard Shortbread Cookies (page 197)

vanilla
Sugar
Butter AA
Butter AA

COOKIE SCIENCE

I often hear the phrase "Cooking is an art; baking is a science." While I do think there is a lot of art in baking as well, it really is a science. Baking requires precision and technique because chemical reactions are key to successful baked goods. And half of baking success is just understanding your ingredients and what they do. I want you to understand the ins and outs of cookies so you can make the best cookies possible. I want you to know what baking powder does and why we are adding it to a cookie. I want you to know how to measure flour and understand what happens when you do it incorrectly. But don't worry, we're not going to get too technical here. This isn't a college-level nutrition course—I won't be breaking down monosaccharides or explaining the complexity of protein coagulation, but I want you to know the basics. I want you to understand what each ingredient is, what it does in a cookie, and how you can use it to control your cookie result. When you finish this chapter, you'll be ready to master any cookie in this book!

BUTTER

Oh, butter. I love butter with all my heart.

Butter is made by churning cream until the fat (solid butter) separates from the liquid (buttermilk). Standard American butter is made up of around 80 to 82 percent butterfat; the other components are water (typically 16 to 18 percent) and milk solids (1 to 2 percent).

Butter is crucial in cookies. It affects flavor, texture, spread, and structure. Where would we be without it?

- **Flavor:** Butter adds a rich, creamy taste to cookies. When butter is browned (more on this on the next page), it develops a toasted, nutty flavor.
- **Texture:** Because butter is a fat, it tenderizes cookie dough by coating flour proteins, which limits gluten development (too much gluten = tough cookies). Creaming butter also incorporates air into the dough, making cookies lighter and fluffier.
- **Spread:** When butter melts in the oven, it causes cookie dough to spread out. As the chart below shows, butter temperature affects how much cookies spread.
- **Structure:** The fat in butter solidifies as cookies cool, helping them hold their shape.

Butter Temperature	Result in Cookies	Why It Happens
Cold	Thick, chewy cookies with minimal spread	Minimal air is incorporated during mixing; butter melts slowly in the oven
Softened	Light, tender cookies with moderate/even spread	Softened butter is best for creaming, which incorporates air into the dough, creating lift and fluffiness
Melted	Thin, chewy, dense cookies with more spread	No air is incorporated during mixing; butter is already liquified when it bakes

BROWN BUTTER

It's no secret that I am obsessed with brown butter. There are few better-tasting things in the world. I love it in my cookies and in any kind of baked good, really (or any savory thing, for that matter). Though I do so adore brown butter, it does not belong in every cookie. But if you are on a hunt for that delicious nutty flavor, here are all the brown butter cookies in the book:

- Brown Butter CCC (page 60)
- Masa Harina CCC (page 67)
- White Chocolate Macadamia Nut Cookies (page 88)
- Rice Krispies Treat Cookies (page 162)
- Small-Batch Brown Butter CCC (page 205)
- Cinnamon and Milk Chocolate Cookies with Hazelnut Cream Filling (page 224)
- Pistachio Cream Stuffed Cookies (page 244)

Let's dive into what exactly brown butter is: Brown butter, also called beurre noisette (which means "hazelnut butter" in French) is butter that has been simmered until it turns brown in color and develops a rich, nutty aroma. But what is actually happening in that process?

As we learned earlier, 1 to 2 percent of butter is milk solids. These milk solids are neither fat nor water but are primarily made up of proteins, lactose, and minerals. In a stick of butter, these solids are dispersed throughout the fat. But when butter is melted and simmered in a pan, most of the water evaporates, and the milk solids separate from the fat and sink to the bottom of the pan, where they toast and turn brown. The browned milk solids create that deep, nutty flavor. It's magical!

If you have never made brown butter before, don't be intimidated! It's so easy—after you make it once, you'll be a master.

SALTED VS. UNSALTED BUTTER

Now we enter the heated debate of salted vs. unsalted butter. Traditionally, unsalted butter is the standard go-to in baking. It's argued to be superior because it allows you to control the amount of salt in your baked goods. I understand the argument, but I respectfully disagree. I am fully on team salted butter in baked goods. Let me tell you why.

- Baked goods are often undersalted, making them too sweet. Cookies especially need the balance provided by salt for all the flavors to shine (more on this later), and a lot of cookies just fall short (*cough cough* major cookie franchises). Especially in the home kitchen, undersalting is a far more prevalent cookie issue than oversalting, so using salted butter helps us avoid that problem.
- I'm not the only one on this side of the butter argument. Jessie Sheehan, cookbook author and baking podcast host, said, "When I am baking at home, I prefer salted butter, and not because I want baked goods to taste saltier. It's because I don't want them to taste flat. Salt pops flavor, including chocolate, vanilla, and fruit."

If you only have unsalted butter, that is totally fine! Add an extra ¼ teaspoon salt per ½ cup (113 g) butter and you'll be set. So, use what you have, but if you're going grocery shopping, grab salted!

SUGAR

There are a lot of different types of sugar in the world, but for the purpose of this book, we are focusing on the two most popular kinds: brown sugar and granulated sugar.

First, let's chat about how sugar is made.

Granulated sugar is made from sugarcane or sugar beets. In either case, the process is generally the same and results in pure sucrose (sugar). Juice is extracted from crushed sugarcane or thinly sliced sugar beets and is treated to remove any impurities. The clarified juice is concentrated through a complex boiling and evaporating process and is refined into crystalized sugar. In the final steps, the crystals are removed from the remaining liquid (molasses) in a centrifuge and then are washed and dried, resulting in white (granulated) sugar.

Brown sugar, on the other hand, is made through the same basic process but with a twist at the end. There are two types of brown sugar: *Natural brown sugar* is essentially granulated sugar that doesn't get fully refined, so some molasses remains naturally in the sugar crystals. One example of natural brown sugar is turbinado sugar (which we use in a few recipes in the book!). *Refined brown sugar* is by far the most common type of brown sugar. It follows the same process as granulated sugar, but once the granulated sugar is derived, some molasses is added back in. This process allows manufacturers to precisely control the amount of molasses in the final product.

DARK VS. LIGHT BROWN SUGAR

You've probably seen both *dark* brown sugar and *light* brown sugar at the grocery store. Light brown sugar is more common, but the only difference between the two is the amount of molasses. Light brown sugar generally contains about 3.5 percent molasses, and dark brown sugar contains about 6.5 percent. You can use either for any recipe in this book, but I *strongly* prefer *dark* brown sugar! Thanks to the higher molasses content, dark brown sugar makes cookies even softer and more caramelly, which is always a big yes from me.

Now, let's dive into what sugar does in cookies.

With granulated sugar, cookies spread more and have crispier edges. Why?

- **It melts quickly:** Granulated sugar liquifies easily while baking, which causes cookies to flatten out in the oven and develop a caramelized, crisp crust at the edges.

With brown sugar, cookies become thicker and softer. Why?

- **More acidic:** Molasses is acidic, and as we will learn more about on page 43, leaveners (like baking soda) need an acid to cause the chemical reaction that gives cookies rise. So, cookies with brown sugar will be puffier.
- **More moisture retention:** Brown sugar attracts and retains more water, which helps cookies stay soft and tender.

EGGS

Eggs are both incredibly fascinating and incredibly versatile. They are essential in almost all baking, and they definitely prove their worth in cookies. We all know where eggs come from, so let's break down what they are made of.

A whole egg is mainly made up of (approximately):

- **Water:** 75 percent
- **Protein:** 12.5 percent
- **Fat:** 10 percent

But when we look at egg whites versus egg yolks, the percentages are very different:

Egg white (approximately):

- **Water:** 88 percent
- **Protein:** 11 percent

Egg yolk (approximately):

- **Water:** 55 percent
- **Fat:** 27 percent
- **Protein:** 15 percent

Now, let's go over the main functions of eggs in cookies:

- **Moisture:** Eggs are made mostly of water, so they add moisture to the dough, creating softer, cakier cookies.
- **Structure:** Eggs act as a binding agent in cookies, mainly thanks to the proteins found in both egg whites and yolks. The protein coagulates (turns from a liquid to a solid) as the dough cooks, helping cookies retain their shape and providing structure.
- **Leavening:** Particularly when we're using separated egg whites, beating eggs traps air in the dough, which helps cookies rise slightly.
- **Richness:** Egg yolks have a high amount of fat, which provides decadence and flavor and makes for a denser, chewier cookie.

EGG SUBSTITUTES

There is no perfect substitute for eggs, but if someone you're baking for is vegan or has an allergy, there are a few sub-ins that usually work well in cookies. Disclaimer: None of the recipes in this book have been tested with any of these substitutes, so I can't ensure the results. But I have tried all the following egg substitutes side by side in chocolate chip cookies, and while there were small differences in taste, texture, and appearance, the cookies were all delicious! So, if you find yourself in need of an egg substitute, feel confident trying one of these:

- **Flax egg:** Combine 3 tablespoons water with 1 tablespoon ground flaxseed in a bowl. Let it set up for 5 minutes and then it's ready to use. The gelatinous mixture works similarly to eggs as a binding agent.
- **Egg replacer powder:** Sold by a handful of brands at most grocery stores (I like Bob's Red Mill), egg replacer powder is typically made of a combination of starches and leaveners. When mixed with water, it creates a gelatinous binding agent similar to a flax egg. The added leaveners also help replicate the slight lift that eggs provide in cookies.
- **Yogurt:** Use 3 to 4 tablespoons plain yogurt (or soy yogurt for a vegan option) in place of an egg. Similarly to eggs, yogurt contains protein and fat and provides moisture.

FLOUR

Flour is the backbone of all baked goods, providing essential structure and texture.

We get flour by grinding grains, nuts, seeds, legumes, or even some fruits and vegetables. Wheat is overwhelmingly the most popular base for flour, but rye, corn, and buckwheat (among many other options) also produce flours that can be delicious additions to cookies. Most of the cookies in this book use all-purpose flour, which is a refined wheat flour, but a handful use other flours like corn-based masa harina or rye flour.

We'll also use other wheat flours, like bread flour and whole wheat flour, which differ from all-purpose in their protein content. Remember: More protein means more gluten-forming potential, and more gluten equals a stronger, chewier structure. The chart below shows how the protein content of each kind of flour impacts the texture of our cookies.

Type	Protein Content	Texture in Cookie
All-purpose flour	9 to 12 percent	Balanced: chewy and tender
Bread flour	12 to 14 percent	Extra chewy
Whole wheat flour	11 to 15 percent	Dense and hearty
Rye flour	7 to 9 percent	Soft, chewy, and tender
Masa harina	6 to 8 percent	Slightly gritty and cornmeal-like
Almond flour	20 to 24 percent	Grainy, delicate crumb

WORKING WITH FLOUR

YOU NEED A KITCHEN SCALE! OK, OK, that sounds dramatic, but just hear me out: I've been sharing cookie recipes online for years, and every once in a while, I get a comment from a reader that their cookies didn't spread like they were supposed to. My first question always is "How did you measure your flour?" Depending on how you add flour to a measuring cup, 1 cup of all-purpose flour can weigh anywhere from 110 to 170 grams. For this book, we are measuring 1 cup of flour as 130 grams. If you pack your flour into your measuring cup and then level it off (the way I always measured flour growing up), you'll land close to 170 grams. That additional 40 grams will almost always make your cookies too dry and crumbly. The easiest way to avoid the inconsistency? *Use a scale.* That way, you can measure precisely every time. If you refuse (I'll be disappointed, but we can still be friends), then the next-best method is using a spoon to lightly scoop flour into your measuring cup and gently scraping any excess off the top. This should put you close to 130 grams per cup every time. (Once you add flour to a cookie dough, make sure you never overmix. Overmixing the dough incorporates too much air and develops the gluten in the flour. This results in a denser, tougher texture instead of a softer, chewier one.)

ALTITUDE

Where you live can really affect how your baked goods turn out. Crazy, right? If you live at a high altitude (above 3,000 feet/900 meters), you might need to make adjustments here and there for your cookies to turn out just right.

This is because at high altitudes, the air pressure is lower and the air is drier, which causes cookies to rise more quickly and potentially collapse, meaning they will spread more. To combat this, you can add 1 to 2 additional tablespoons of flour per cup to reinforce the cookies' structure. Granted, while altitude can have a significant impact on baked goods with long rising and baking times (like bread), it shouldn't make a huge difference with cookies. During the testing process of the recipes in this book, I had one official recipe tester at sea level and one at a high altitude, both making the same recipes. There wasn't much of a difference between the cookies that each tester made, so you shouldn't need to adjust much. If you notice they aren't working quite right, though, try adding a bit more flour.

LEAVENERS

Nearly all baked goods use some type of leavener.

A leavener is an ingredient that causes a dough or batter to rise, typically by producing carbon dioxide (CO_2). There are three main types of leaveners: biological, mechanical, and chemical.

- **Biological leaveners:** Living organisms, primarily yeast, produce CO_2 over time through fermentation, giving lift to breads and other baked goods.
- **Mechanical leaveners:** This doesn't refer to specific ingredients but rather to the physical incorporation of air into dough or batter. Think creaming butter and sugar together or whipping egg whites. The trapped air bubbles expand during baking and help provide a lighter, fluffier texture.
- **Chemical leaveners:** These work by reacting with heat, moisture, or acid to release CO_2. Baking soda and baking powder are the most prevalent chemical leaveners used in cookies, and to understand how they work, we're going to dive in deep.

BAKING SODA

Baking soda (also known as sodium bicarbonate) needs an acidic ingredient to activate, like brown sugar, yogurt, or lemon juice. When combined with an acid, it reacts by releasing CO_2, causing the dough to rise.

What it does in cookies:

- Helps cookies spread and brown
- Forms crispier edges
- Creates a chewier interior

BAKING POWDER

Baking powder is a combination of things: baking soda, an acid (usually cream of tartar), and a buffering agent (usually cornstarch to keep it dry and stable). Unlike baking soda, baking powder already has the acid it needs to activate, so it kick-starts all on its own. Double-acting baking powder (the most common) reacts in two stages: first when it is mixed with a liquid and again when it's exposed to heat.

What it does in cookies:

- Creates a lighter, puffier cookie
- Results in a cakier texture

WHY DO SO MANY COOKIE RECIPES USE BOTH?

Many cookie recipes (including several in this book) use a combination of baking soda and baking powder. Using both gives you the best of both worlds: a cookie that spreads and browns on the edges while being soft and slightly puffy in the middle. Depending on the texture and appearance you want, you can adjust these two leaveners to get your perfect cookie!

KEEPING LEAVENERS FRESH

When baking soda and baking powder are past their prime, they become less reactive, resulting in subpar cookies. As a rule of thumb, you should replace them every 8 to 12 months. Here's how to check if yours are still fresh:

- **Baking soda:** Mix it with vinegar—if it's still fresh, it will fizz.
- **Baking powder:** Mix it with hot water—if it's still fresh, it will bubble.

SALT

My love for salt runs deep. You will catch me throwing one pinch of salt into my food and another straight into my mouth.

I got it from my mama: She is obsessed with salt and always has been. And while salt is very important to me, it is *definitely* very important in cookies. Salt not only is essential for flavor but also helps with browning, strengthens gluten, and helps retain moisture. A cookie without salt is just about the only cookie I don't want.

The type of salt you use actually matters a lot. Different types of salt vary in texture, crystal size, and saltiness (per volume), which can have a huge impact. These are the most common types of salt used in baking and how they compare.

MY FAVORITE KIND OF SALT

For all the recipes in this book, I use Diamond Crystal Kosher Salt. It's the go-to for most professional chefs and a lot of home cooks and bakers, and if you've never used it before, I think you'll be hooked after one try.

Diamond Crystal is so well loved because it gives you way more control. Its clean flavor, light texture, and low salinity make it forgiving and precise. That's especially important in baking, where small differences can have big effects. Its hollow crystals also dissolve quickly, helping the salt seamlessly integrate into your dough without leaving a gritty residue or extra-salty pockets.

If you still aren't convinced and are intent on using table salt, *please* adjust the salt amount down: For each recipe, if using table salt, you should cut the amount of salt in half. If not, you'll bake your way through this book thinking I am even more obsessed with salt than I am.

Type and Grain	Salinity	Additives	Salting Notes
Table salt Uniform, very small grains	Most salty by volume	Contains iodine and usually an anti-caking agent (keeps salt from clumping together)	Because the grain size is so fine, it's easy to oversalt your food if substituting table salt for more coarse salts. Iodized salt can also sometimes create a slight metallic flavor in baked goods.
Kosher salt Irregularly shaped coarse flakes	About half as salty as table salt by volume	Usually additive-free	Even kosher salts can vary! Morton Coarse Kosher Salt is denser than Diamond Crystal Kosher Salt, so they are not interchangeable 1:1. The saltiness ratio is closer to 2:1 (Morton:Diamond).
Flake salt Extra-large flat flakes	Much less salty than table salt by volume (thanks to the big, airy crystals)	Usually additive-free	Flake salt is most commonly used as a finishing salt rather than an ingredient in the dough. I love a sprinkle of flaky salt on almost all of my cookies for an extra salty kick with each bite.

CHOCOLATE

OK, I know I just gushed about my love for salt, but omg, chocolate. I've always loved it.

My parents' house was definitely an "ingredients household" (read: not very snacky), so one of my favorite treats was a handful of chocolate chips (which I would sneak multiple times a day). These days, I'm unfortunately—or actually, fortunately—one of those people who needs a sweet treat after every meal, and I still find myself reaching for that handful of chocolate chips. I guess old habits die hard.

If you aren't a chocolate person, don't worry: There are so many recipes in this book that are chocolate-free and totally delicious. But for those of us who love our cookies chock-full of chocolatey goodness, let's explore the various types of chocolate we will use in this book.

Type	Cocoa Percentage	Sweetness	Flavor Profile
White chocolate	0 percent cocoa solids, but 20 to 40 percent cocoa butter	Very sweet	Milky, buttery, with notes of vanilla
Caramelized white chocolate	0 percent cocoa solids, but 20 to 40 percent cocoa butter	Sweet	Nutty, toasty, almost caramellike
Milk chocolate	10 to 50 percent	Sweet	Creamy, mellow cocoa flavor, with notes of milk and vanilla
Semisweet chocolate	35 to 60 percent	Moderately sweet	Balanced sweetness and rich cocoa flavor
Dark chocolate	35 to 100 percent*	Slightly sweet	Bold, intense cocoa flavor

*Most dark chocolate is 60 percent cocoa or greater.

We also have to consider chocolate chips versus chocolate chunks. They can be used pretty interchangeably in this book, but each results in a different outcome. Chocolate chips typically have additives like soy lecithin and paraffin wax. These stabilizers help chocolate chips hold their shape during baking by resisting melting at typical oven temperatures. Chocolate chunks, on the other hand, contain few to no stabilizers, so they will melt more readily in the oven, losing their shape. You can buy chocolate chunks premade or chop up a chocolate bar. I've done both, but I typically opt to chop up a bar so I can get a variety of sizes (and reserve the big chunks to press into the top of each dough ball for a gorgeous pool of chocolate on top). I will direct you in each recipe as to whether I want you to use chocolate chips or chunks, but here's a general breakdown for when you'd want to use each one.

Chocolate Chips

- Maintaining defined chocolate chip shapes once baked
- Consistent, neat, uniform-looking cookies
- Even distribution of chocolate throughout each cookie

Chocolate Chunks

- More "gourmet" or rustic appearance
- Varied texture and gooey pools of chocolate
- Melty ribbons of chocolate throughout each cookie

COOKIE CHECKLIST

I just made a cookie, and it didn't turn out like the photo. What did I do wrong?

SPREAD TOO MUCH?

- Not enough flour
- Butter too warm
- Dough wasn't chilled

DIDN'T SPREAD ENOUGH?

- Too much flour
- Butter too cold
- Dough too chilled

TOO SALTY?

- Are you using Diamond Crystal Kosher Salt? If you are using regular table salt or Morton Coarse Kosher Salt, divide all the salt amounts in half.

TOO CRUNCHY?

- In the oven for too long

BURNING ON THE BOTTOM?

- Oven runs hot—buy an oven thermometer
- Using dark-colored baking sheets—light-colored baking sheets will ensure more even baking

NOT RISING?

- Old or expired baking soda or baking powder (see instructions on page 43 to test for expiration)

TOO TOUGH?

- Dough was overmixed (gluten is overdeveloped)

CHOCOLATE CHIP COOKIES (CCC): HAVE IT YOUR WAY

"How do you like your chocolate chip cookie?" is one of the most divisive questions of all time. Everyone likes their CCC a little bit different: thick and gooey (page 55), crunchy edges with a soft middle (page 52), thin and crispy (page 56)—the list goes on. This chapter has eleven different chocolate chip cookie recipes, so everyone can have it their way! From classic CCC (plus Brown Butter CCC on page 60) to more inventive options like Masa Harina CCC (page 67) and Spicy CCC (page 71), this chapter truly has something for everyone.

CRUNCHY EDGE, SOFT MIDDLE CCC

Oh, the humble crunchy edge, soft middle CCC. Arguably the *chocolate chip cookie. If you ask someone what they expect a chocolate chip cookie to look and taste like, this is probably it. These cookies come together in one bowl, without a mixer, so they're the perfect go-to CCC. I highly recommend chilling the dough for 12 hours before baking, as it allows for the flour to fully hydrate and the butter to cool down so your cookies don't spread too much. But if you're absolutely in a pinch, you can throw the dough balls in the freezer for a couple hours and call it good. As for the chocolate, use whatever speaks to you—a mix of milk and dark chocolate is always my combination of choice.*

MAKES 8 LARGE COOKIES

½ cup (113 g) salted butter, melted
½ cup (108 g) brown sugar
⅓ cup (66 g) granulated sugar
1 large egg, room temperature
1½ teaspoons vanilla extract
1¼ cups (162 g) all-purpose flour
1 teaspoon Diamond Crystal kosher salt
½ teaspoon baking soda
¾ cups (128 g) milk and/or dark chocolate chunks, plus extra for topping
Flaky salt, for topping

1. Place the butter, brown sugar, and granulated sugar in a large bowl. Use a whisk or rubber spatula to mix until well combined, about 2 minutes.
2. Add the egg and vanilla extract. Mix until combined, about 1 minute.
3. Add the flour, kosher salt, and baking soda. Use a rubber spatula to mix until the flour is just incorporated, about 1 minute.
4. Add the chocolate chunks and mix until evenly distributed through the dough.
5. Use a large (4-tablespoon/2-ounce) cookie scoop to scoop the dough into balls. Top each dough ball with one or two chunks of chocolate, gently pressing the chunks into the dough. Place all the dough balls onto a small baking sheet or plate lined with parchment paper. Cover and transfer to the fridge to chill overnight (or for at least 12 hours; see Note 1 on page 55).
6. Preheat the oven to 350°F (180°C). Line two baking sheets with parchment paper.
7. Place four dough balls onto each baking sheet, spaced equally apart. Bake for 12 to 15 minutes, until the edges are golden brown.
8. Top each cookie with a pinch of flaky salt. Let the cookies cool on the baking sheets for 15 minutes and then transfer to a cooling rack to cool completely.

THICK AND GOOEY CCC

I couldn't write a whole chapter about CCC and not include a thick and gooey CCC. There is something about us (well, most of us) that makes us love a slightly underbaked, baseball-sized cookie that still tastes like cookie dough. Some may wonder why we don't just eat straight dough instead (that recipe is on page 72), but there's something about the golden brown, crunchy exterior combined with the gooey, cookie dough–esque interior of these cookies that is just magic.

MAKES 5 EXTRA-LARGE COOKIES

½ cup (113 g) salted butter, cold

¾ cup (160 g) brown sugar

¼ cup (50 g) granulated sugar

1 large egg

1 teaspoon vanilla extract

2 cups (260 g) all-purpose flour

1½ teaspoons baking powder

1 teaspoon Diamond Crystal kosher salt

½ teaspoon baking soda

1½ cups (255 g) milk and/or semisweet chocolate chips

1. Cut the butter into 1-inch (2.5 cm) cubes. Place the cubed butter, brown sugar, and granulated sugar in a large bowl. Use a stand mixer or hand mixer to mix until the butter is broken down and just combined with the sugar, about 2 minutes.
2. Add the egg and vanilla extract. Mix until just combined with no visible streaks of egg, about 1 minute.
3. Add the flour, baking powder, salt, and baking soda. Mix on low until the flour is almost combined, about 30 seconds.
4. Add the chocolate chips and mix just until no streaks of flour remain and the chocolate chips are evenly distributed throughout the dough.
5. Use a kitchen scale to divide the dough into five 6-ounce (170 g/about ¾ cup) dough balls. Place the dough balls in an airtight container and transfer to the fridge to chill overnight (or for at least 12 hours; see Note 1).
6. Preheat the oven to 375°F (190°C). Line a baking sheet with parchment paper. Place the dough balls on the baking sheet, spaced equally apart.
7. Bake for 12 to 15 minutes, until the tops are a deep golden brown and the edges are just set (they will still be very gooey on the inside; see Note 2). Let the cookies cool on the baking sheet for 15 minutes and then transfer to a cooling rack to cool completely.

NOTES

1. Chilling the cookies in the fridge is best, but if you can't wait overnight, put them in the freezer for 2 hours instead.

2. These cookies are designed to be undercooked. We bake them at a higher temperature, so the outside gets really beautifully cooked but the inside stays nice and gooey. You can eat these before they're completely cooled, but the inside will be really gooey, so I recommend waiting for them to cool. But if you dive in early, I won't tell anyone—your secret is safe with me.

THIN AND CRISPY CCC

If you love crunchy cookies, this recipe is for you. Admittedly, these would never be my first choice of CCC. I am a sucker for a thick, soft cookie (as is probably evident in most of the recipes in this book). But I will say, there are times when all I want is something sweet and crunchy, and these cookies are the perfect fix. Melting the butter and adding less flour are the main ways we're achieving such thin cookies here, and a longer bake time gets us that golden brown, crispy crunch.

MAKES 18 MEDIUM COOKIES

½ cup (113 g) salted butter, melted
½ cup (100 g) granulated sugar
¼ cup (54 g) brown sugar
1 large egg, room temperature
1 teaspoon vanilla extract
1 cup (130 g) all-purpose flour
½ teaspoon baking soda
½ teaspoon Diamond Crystal kosher salt
½ cup (85 g) semisweet chocolate chips

1. Preheat the oven to 350°F (180°C). Line two baking sheets with parchment paper.
2. Place the butter, granulated sugar, and brown sugar in a large bowl. Use a stand mixer, hand mixer, or whisk to mix until well combined, about 2 minutes.
3. Add the egg and vanilla extract. Mix until combined, about 1 minute.
4. Add the flour, baking soda, and salt. Mix on low until just combined, about 30 seconds.
5. Use a medium (2-tablespoon/1-ounce) cookie scoop to scoop the dough into balls. Place five or six chocolate chips on top of each dough ball.
6. Place up to six dough balls onto each baking sheet, spaced equally apart. (They will spread a lot!)
7. Bake for 12 to 14 minutes, until the cookies are deeply golden brown. Let the cookies cool on the baking sheets for 10 minutes and then transfer to a cooling rack to cool completely.
8. Repeat step 7 to bake the remaining dough balls.

NOTE

If you don't like the look of the chocolate chips on top, you can add ¼ cup (42 g) chocolate chips to the batter and gently mix them in before scooping the dough into balls.

OATMEAL CCC

I am a big fan of oats in cookies. Not only do they add great texture, but they also make cookies soft—and keep them soft. And who doesn't love a soft cookie? If you want to take these cookies to the next level, try toasting the oats before adding them to the dough. Place the oats on an unlined baking sheet and bake at 350°F (180°C) for about 10 minutes, until they begin to brown. Let the oats cool completely before adding them to the dough. Browning the oats brings out a sort of nutty, toasty flavor that really makes these cookies shine.

MAKES 8 LARGE COOKIES

¾ cup (162 g) brown sugar
½ cup (113 g) salted butter, softened
1 large egg, room temperature
1 teaspoon vanilla extract
1¼ cups (162 g) all-purpose flour
1 cup (90 g) rolled oats
1 teaspoon Diamond Crystal kosher salt
½ teaspoon baking powder
½ teaspoon baking soda
½ cup (85 g) semisweet chocolate chips

1. Preheat the oven to 350°F (180°C). Line two baking sheets with parchment paper.
2. Place the brown sugar and butter in a large bowl. Use a stand mixer or hand mixer to mix until well combined, about 2 minutes.
3. Add the egg and vanilla extract and mix until fluffy and lighter in color, about 1 minute.
4. Add the flour, oats, salt, baking powder, and baking soda. Mix on low until just combined, about 30 seconds.
5. Add the chocolate chips and mix on low until evenly distributed throughout the dough.
6. Use a large (4-tablespoon/2-ounce) cookie scoop to scoop the dough into balls. Place up to four dough balls onto each baking sheet, spaced equally apart.
7. Bake for 8 to 11 minutes, until the edges are just starting to set. The centers should still look slightly underbaked. Let the cookies cool on the baking sheets for 10 minutes and then transfer to a cooling rack to cool completely.

BROWN BUTTER CCC

Dare I say there is nothing better than a brown butter chocolate chip cookie? I still remember the day I used brown butter in a chocolate chip cookie for the first time, and my life has never been the same. There is something about nutty brown butter + brown sugar + melty pools of chocolate that does it for me every time. These BB CCCs (as I affectionately refer to them) are crispy on the outside, chewy on the inside, and topped with plenty of flaky salt. The overnight rest is crucial for the texture, but waiting is definitely the hardest part!

MAKES 8 LARGE COOKIES

½ cup (113 g) salted butter, cubed
1 small ice cube
½ cup (108 g) brown sugar
¼ cup (50 g) granulated sugar
1 large egg, room temperature
1 teaspoon vanilla extract
1¼ cups (162 g) all-purpose flour
½ tablespoon cornstarch
½ teaspoon baking soda
¾ teaspoon Diamond Crystal kosher salt
¾ cup (128 g) chocolate chunks (milk, semisweet, dark, or a mix), plus extra for topping (see Note 1)
Flaky salt, for topping

NOTES

1. Feel free to use chocolate chips instead of chunks! You won't have the same pools of melted chocolate in and on top of the cookie, but chips will get the job done.

2. The overnight rest is crucial for these cookies. It allows the brown butter flavor to fully seep into the dough and prevents the cookies from spreading too much.

3. After the overnight rest, bake these cookies straight from the fridge! Don't let the dough come up to room temperature, or the cookies will spread too much.

1. Heat a large pan over medium heat. Add the butter and stir until melted, about 1 minute. Keep stirring as the melted butter starts to bubble and then foam, about 2 minutes. After the foam subsides, you'll see brown flecks on the bottom of the pan, and the butter will smell very nutty. Pour the brown butter into a small heat-safe bowl, add the ice cube, and stir until the ice cube melts. Let the butter cool to room temperature. (If you are in a hurry, cover the bowl with plastic wrap or a lid and transfer to the fridge or freezer to speed up the process.)
2. Transfer the butter to a large bowl with the brown sugar and granulated sugar. Using a stand mixer or hand mixer, mix until fluffy and lighter in color, about 2 minutes.
3. Add the egg and vanilla extract. Mix until combined, about 1 minute.
4. Add the flour, cornstarch, baking soda, and kosher salt. Mix until just combined, about 30 seconds.
5. Add the chocolate chunks and mix until evenly distributed through the dough.
6. Line a baking sheet with parchment paper. Use a large (4-tablespoon/2-ounce) cookie scoop to scoop the dough into balls. Top each dough ball with one or two chunks of chocolate, gently pressing the chunks into the dough.
7. Cover the pan with plastic wrap and then place in the fridge and let the dough chill for at least 12 hours or up to 72 hours (see Note 2).
8. To bake the cookies (see Note 3), preheat the oven to 350°F (180°C). Line two baking sheets with parchment paper.

9. Transfer up to four dough balls onto each baking sheet, spaced equally apart. Bake for 10 to 12 minutes, until the edges of the cookies are just starting to brown. Let the cookies cool on the baking sheets for 10 minutes and then transfer to a cooling rack to cool completely (or enjoy hot for an ooey-gooey cookie!). Top each cookie with a pinch of flaky salt.

OLIVE OIL CCC

Olive oil and chocolate chip cookies isn't usually the first combination that comes to mind, but trust me when I say it's a combination that works. Olive oil is used in place of butter in this recipe, creating a moister cookie that is dense and has a rich flavor from the floral notes of the oil. Olive oil also creates a cookie with a less chewy texture than butter does, so I use bread flour instead of all-purpose (bread flour has a higher protein content, resulting in a chewier texture). This results in a rich, unique CCC that is still soft and tender.

MAKES 9 LARGE COOKIES

⅔ cup (144 g) brown sugar

½ cup (120 ml) olive oil

⅓ cup (66 g) granulated sugar

1 large egg, room temperature

1 teaspoon vanilla extract

1½ cups (195 g) bread flour (see Note)

1 teaspoon Diamond Crystal kosher salt

½ teaspoon baking soda

1 cup (170 g) semisweet chocolate chunks, plus extra for topping

1. Preheat the oven to 350°F (180°C). Line two baking sheets with parchment paper.
2. Place the brown sugar, olive oil, and granulated sugar in a large bowl. Whisk until well combined, about 1 minute.
3. Add the egg and vanilla extract and mix again until the oil is fully incorporated, about 1 minute.
4. Add the flour, salt, and baking soda. Use a rubber spatula to mix just until no streaks of flour remain, about 1 minute. Add the chocolate chunks and mix until evenly distributed through the dough.
5. Use a large (4-tablespoon/2-ounce) cookie scoop to scoop the dough into balls. Place up to five dough balls onto each baking sheet, spaced equally apart. Top each dough ball with one or two chunks of chocolate, gently pressing them in.
6. Bake for 10 to 13 minutes, until the edges are just starting to brown. Let the cookies cool on the baking sheets for 10 minutes and then transfer to a cooling rack to cool completely.

NOTE

If you don't have bread flour, use all-purpose flour instead.

FROSTED AND CHILLED CCC

I know I may have lost some of you after you read the name of this cookie, but trust me here, and let me set the stage: We start with a soft oatmeal cookie with a generous amount of milk chocolate chips. The cookies are baked at a low temperature and then placed directly into the fridge so they set up quickly. This keeps the cookies incredibly soft. We then top them with a smooth buttercream frosting and pop them back into the fridge. They're best enjoyed cold, and since they're so soft, biting into them is a delightful experience. So, I hope I've convinced you, and if not, try it anyway—I'll let the recipe do the talking.

MAKES 7 LARGE COOKIES

CCC Dough

½ cup (113 g) salted butter, cold
⅓ cup (72 g) brown sugar
¼ cup (50 g) granulated sugar
1 large egg
1 teaspoon vanilla extract
1¼ cups (162 g) all-purpose flour
½ cup (45 g) rolled oats
¾ teaspoon Diamond Crystal kosher salt
¼ teaspoon baking powder
⅔ cup (113 g) milk chocolate chips

Buttercream Frosting

¼ cup (56 g) salted butter, softened
1 cup (113 g) powdered sugar, sifted
1 to 2 tablespoons heavy cream or milk, room temperature
1 teaspoon vanilla extract
Pinch of Diamond Crystal kosher salt

NOTE

These cookies are best served chilled! Keep them in the fridge until serving.

1. Preheat the oven to 325°F (165°C). Line two baking sheet with parchment paper.
2. Make the cookies: Cut the butter into ½-inch (1 cm) cubes and then transfer to a large bowl. Add the brown sugar and granulated sugar. Use a stand mixer or hand mixer to mix until combined, about 3 minutes.
3. Add the egg and vanilla extract and mix until combined, about 1 minute.
4. Add the flour, oats, salt, and baking powder. Mix on low until just combined, about 30 seconds.
5. Add the chocolate chips and mix on low until evenly distributed throughout the dough.
6. Use a large (4-tablespoon/2-ounce) cookie scoop to scoop the dough into balls. Place up to four dough balls onto each baking sheet, spaced equally apart. Use the palm of your hand to slightly flatten each dough ball into a cylinder shape (so the ball is about 1 inch/2.5 cm tall).
7. Bake for 10 to 12 minutes, until the edges are just starting to set. The middle will still look slightly doughy. Immediately transfer the cookies to a plate lined with parchment paper, transfer to the fridge, and let cool completely, about 30 minutes.
8. Meanwhile, make the frosting: Place the butter in a medium bowl. Use a stand mixer or hand mixer to mix until creamy, about 2 minutes.
9. Add the powdered sugar, 1 tablespoon heavy cream, the vanilla extract, and the salt. Mix on low for 1 minute and then on high until smooth, about 2 minutes. If the frosting is too thick and not spreadable, add another tablespoon of heavy cream.

10. When the cookies are completely cool, use a small offset spatula to spread 2 tablespoons of frosting on each cookie in an even layer. Transfer the cookies back to the fridge to chill for at least 15 minutes before eating (see Note on page 64).

MASA HARINA CCC

If you think you've never had masa harina, think again. "Masa harina" literally translates to "dough flour," and it's the type of flour used for corn tortillas and tamales. It is made from dried corn kernels that are treated through a process called nixtamalization, which involves soaking the kernels in a solution of water and calcium hydroxide. The nixtamalization process softens the corn's tough outer skin and creates a slightly sour flavor. After soaking, the kernels are rinsed, dried, and ground into a fine powder, making masa harina. It gives these cookies a somewhat tangy flavor, but nothing too overbearing. The corn tortilla taste is there, but the dark chocolate chunks and brown butter bring these firmly into CCC flavor territory. The result is a beautiful balance that I think you will love.

MAKES 7 LARGE COOKIES

½ cup (113 g) salted butter, softened

½ cup (100 g) granulated sugar

¼ cup (54 g) brown sugar

1 large egg plus 1 large egg yolk, room temperature

1 teaspoon vanilla extract

¾ cup (98 g) all-purpose flour

⅓ cup (31 g) white masa harina (see Note)

1 teaspoon baking soda

1 teaspoon Diamond Crystal kosher salt

1 cup (170 g) dark chocolate chunks, plus extra for topping

Flaky salt, for topping

1. Heat a large pan over medium heat. Add the butter and stir until melted, about 2 minutes. Keep stirring as the melted butter starts to bubble and then foam, 5 to 7 minutes. After the foam subsides, you'll see brown flecks on the bottom of the pan, and the butter will smell very nutty. Pour the brown butter into a small heat-safe bowl and transfer to the freezer to chill for about 10 minutes, until the butter is cool to the touch.
2. Preheat the oven to 350°F (180°C). Line two baking sheets with parchment paper.
3. Place the cooled butter, granulated sugar, and brown sugar in a large bowl. Use a stand mixer or hand mixer to mix until fully combined, about 2 minutes.
4. Add the egg, egg yolk, and vanilla. Mix until combined, about 1 minute.
5. Add the flour, masa harina, baking soda, and kosher salt. Mix on low until just combined.
6. Add the chocolate chunks and mix until evenly distributed through the dough.
7. Use a large (4-tablespoon/2-ounce) cookie scoop to scoop the dough into balls. Place up to four dough balls onto each baking sheet, spaced equally apart. Top each dough ball with a chunk of chocolate, gently pressing it into the dough.
8. Bake for 9 to 11 minutes, until the edges are just set and golden brown. Top each cookie with a pinch of flaky salt. Let the cookies cool on the baking sheets for 10 minutes and then transfer to a cooling rack to cool completely.

NOTE

If you don't have access to masa harina, you can use corn flour (not to be confused with cornstarch) instead.

TAHINI CCC

I am convinced that tahini belongs in cookies. Unlike peanut butter, which has a very overbearing taste (don't worry, I still love you, PB), tahini is much milder. It gives these cookies a slight nutty flavor that elevates them above your average CCC. And tahini + dark chocolate = a match made in heaven. The two work together to make what is maybe my favorite CCC of all time. Everyone you serve these cookies to may not be able to guess that tahini is the secret ingredient, but they will be begging you for this recipe.

MAKES 14 LARGE COOKIES

½ cup (113 g) salted butter, cold
¾ cup (162 g) brown sugar
½ cup (100 g) granulated sugar
½ cup (130 g) tahini
2 large eggs
1 teaspoon vanilla extract
2½ cups (325 g) all-purpose flour
1 teaspoon baking soda
1 teaspoon ground cinnamon
1 teaspoon Diamond Crystal kosher salt
1 cup (170 g) dark chocolate chunks, plus extra for topping
Flaky salt, for topping

1. Preheat the oven to 350°F (180°C). Line two baking sheets with parchment paper.
2. Cut the butter into ½-inch (1 cm) cubes and then transfer to a large bowl. Add the brown sugar and granulated sugar. Use a stand mixer or hand mixer to mix until fully combined, about 2 minutes.
3. Add the tahini, eggs, and vanilla extract. Mix until fully combined, about 2 minutes.
4. Add the flour, baking soda, cinnamon, and kosher salt. Mix on low just until almost combined with no streaks of flour remaining, about 30 seconds.
5. Add the chocolate chunks and mix until the chocolate is evenly distributed through the dough.
6. Use a large (4-tablespoon/2-ounce) cookie scoop to scoop the dough into balls. Place up to four dough balls onto each baking sheet, spaced equally apart. Top each dough ball with one or two chunks of chocolate, gently pressing the chunks into the dough. Bake for 8 to 11 minutes, until the edges are just set.
7. Top each cookie with a pinch of flaky salt. Let the cookies cool on the baking sheets for 10 minutes and then transfer to a cooling rack to cool completely.
8. Repeat steps 6 and 7 to bake the remaining dough.

NOTE

Substitute the tahini with natural peanut butter for an easy peanut butter chocolate chip cookie!

SPICY CCC

At this point, you've seen a lot of different chocolate chip cookies in this chapter, but this might be the craziest one yet. The beauty of this cookie (and the Hot Honey Cookies on page 118) is that the spiciness isn't totally in your face. It's still a spicy cookie, don't get me wrong, but it has more of a subtle, lingering afterburn that you feel in your mouth once you've swallowed a bite. That's thanks to the cayenne pepper. To make sure this cookie isn't too overwhelming, I've added a touch of cinnamon and used whole wheat flour. These additions give the cookie a heartier, earthier flavor profile that grounds the cayenne pepper and creates a perfectly balanced cookie.

MAKES 12 LARGE COOKIES

1 cup (215 g) brown sugar

¾ cup (170 g) salted butter, softened

3 tablespoons granulated sugar

1 large egg plus 1 large egg yolk, room temperature

2 teaspoons vanilla extract

1 cup (130 g) whole wheat flour

⅔ cup (86 g) all-purpose flour

1 teaspoon baking soda

1 teaspoon Diamond Crystal kosher salt

½ teaspoon ground cinnamon

½ to 1 teaspoon cayenne pepper, plus extra for topping

1½ cups (255 g) semisweet or dark chocolate chunks, plus extra for topping

Flaky salt, for topping

1. Preheat the oven to 350°F (180°C). Line two baking sheets with parchment paper.
2. Place the brown sugar, butter, and granulated sugar in a large bowl. Use a stand mixer or hand mixer to mix until combined, about 2 minutes.
3. Add the egg, egg yolk, and vanilla extract, and mix until fluffy and lighter in color, about 1 minute.
4. Add the whole wheat flour, all-purpose flour, baking soda, kosher salt, cinnamon, and ½ to 1 teaspoon cayenne pepper, depending on how spicy you'd like the cookies to be. Mix on low just until the flour is combined, about 30 seconds.
5. Add the chocolate chunks to the bowl. Mix until the chocolate chunks are evenly distributed through the dough.
6. Use a large (4-tablespoon/2-ounce) cookie scoop to scoop the dough into balls. Place up to six dough balls onto each baking sheet, spaced equally apart. Top each dough ball with one or two chunks of chocolate, gently pressing the chunks into the dough.
7. Bake for 9 to 11 minutes, until the edges start to brown. Top each cookie with a pinch of flaky salt and a dash of extra cayenne pepper, if desired. Let the cookies cool on the baking sheets for 10 minutes and then transfer to a cooling rack to cool completely.

EDIBLE CCC DOUGH

You didn't think I'd write an entire chapter about chocolate chip cookies and not give you a recipe for CCC dough, did you? I am, unfortunately, extremely guilty of having no self-control when it comes to cookie dough. I can probably count on one hand the number of times I've made a batch of cookies and not tasted the dough. It's technically not safe to eat cookie dough because of the raw eggs and flour, so this recipe is designed to be safe to eat, for people who just want to eat the dough (see Note 1). We're using a splash of milk instead of eggs and heat-treating our flour (i.e., heating the flour to kill any bacteria), so it is perfectly safe to eat the whole batch.

MAKES 2 CUPS (ABOUT 550 G)

1¼ cups (162 g) all-purpose flour

½ cup (113 g) salted butter, softened

½ cup (108 g) brown sugar

¼ cup (50 g) granulated sugar

2 tablespoons milk

1 teaspoon vanilla extract

½ teaspoon Diamond Crystal kosher salt

½ cup (85 g) chocolate chips (milk, semisweet, dark, or a mix)

1. Heat-treat the flour (see Note 2): Place the flour in a small microwave-safe bowl. Microwave in 30-second increments until the flour reaches 160°F (71°C) on a food thermometer. Alternatively, you can spread the flour in a thin layer on a baking sheet and bake at 300°F (150°C) for 10 minutes, or until the flour reaches 160°F (71°C). Transfer the flour to a small bowl and let cool completely.
2. Place the butter, brown sugar, and granulated sugar in a medium bowl. Use a stand mixer, hand mixer, or whisk to mix until combined, about 1 minute.
3. Add the milk and vanilla extract and mix until smooth, about 1 minute.
4. Add the flour and salt and mix until just combined, about 1 minute.
5. Add the chocolate chips and mix until just distributed throughout the dough.
6. Store any extra cookie dough in an airtight container in the fridge for up to 1 week.

NOTES

1. This dough will not bake well. It is designed to be eaten raw.

2. Heat-treating the flour can sometimes make it stiffer and clumpier. If that is the case for you, use a sifter to sift the flour into the medium bowl with the other ingredients.

THE CLASSICS

The classics are classics for a reason. These flavors have stood the test of time and have proven their worth, so they get their very own chapter! Here, I present to you not only the classics, but the very best version of each one. They're better than your grandma's (sorry, Grams!), and you'll fall in love with each flavor all over again.

SNICKERDOODLE COOKIES

If you are a fan of thin snickerdoodles that are crispy on the edges, you might be mad at me for this recipe, but if you love them soft and chewy, we may have just become best friends. These snickerdoodles are thick and soft, and they stay soft. Snickerdoodles sometimes contain cream of tartar, which is a dry, acidic powder that gives the cookies a distinct tangy flavor. I don't love the tang (sorry!), so you won't find any cream of tartar in these. But what you will find is a plush cookie that I think you'll love.

MAKES 7 LARGE COOKIES

½ cup (113 g) salted butter, softened

½ cup (108 g) brown sugar

¼ cup (50 g) plus 1 tablespoon granulated sugar, divided

1 large egg, room temperature

1 teaspoon vanilla extract

1⅔ cups (215 g) all-purpose flour

1½ teaspoons cornstarch

1 teaspoon Diamond Crystal kosher salt

½ teaspoon baking soda

1 teaspoon ground cinnamon

1. Preheat the oven to 350°F (180°C). Line two baking sheets with parchment paper.
2. Place the butter, brown sugar, and ¼ cup (50 g) granulated sugar in a large bowl. Use a stand mixer or hand mixer to mix until well combined and lighter in color, about 2 minutes.
3. Add the egg and vanilla extract and mix until combined, about 1 minute.
4. Add the flour, cornstarch, salt, and baking soda. Mix on low until the flour is just incorporated, about 30 seconds.
5. Mix the remaining tablespoon of granulated sugar and the cinnamon in a small bowl.
6. Use a large (4-tablespoon/2-ounce) cookie scoop to scoop the dough into balls. Roll each dough ball in the palms of your hands until smooth and then drop it into the cinnamon sugar and roll to coat.
7. Place up to four dough balls onto each baking sheet, spaced equally apart. Use the palm of your hand to slightly flatten each dough ball. Transfer both sheets to the oven and bake for 8 to 10 minutes, until the edges are just starting to set. The cookies should still look very soft in the middle (see Note).
8. Let the cookies cool on the baking sheets for 10 minutes and then transfer to a cooling rack to cool completely.

NOTE

Don't overbake these! It will make them very dry. Make sure you pull them from the oven when they are still soft in the middle so that when they cool completely, they will be very soft and stay that way. Because no one wants a dry snickerdoodle!

PEANUT BUTTER COOKIES

I've met a lot of peanut butter cookies I haven't liked. Most are dry and crumbly, and I am just not here for that. But I've met a handful of peanut butter cookies that have rocked my world, and this is one of them. It's a soft, tender cookie that is anything but dry. For me, when it comes to peanut butter, more is more, so we are adding peanut butter to the dough and then mixing in peanut (or peanut butter) M&M's for the ultimate peanut butter cookie. If you have a peanut allergy, you should probably just turn the page now and not even read the recipe, because it may be too much PB for your system!

MAKES 10 LARGE COOKIES

¾ cup (162 g) brown sugar

½ cup (113 g) salted butter, cold

¼ cup (68 g) creamy peanut butter

1 large egg

1 teaspoon vanilla extract

1¼ cups (162 g) all-purpose flour

1 tablespoon cornstarch

½ teaspoon baking soda

½ teaspoon Diamond Crystal kosher salt

½ cup (100 g) peanut or peanut butter M&M's (see Note)

1. Preheat the oven to 350°F (180°C). Line two baking sheets with parchment paper.
2. Place the brown sugar, butter, and peanut butter in a large bowl. Use a stand mixer or hand mixer to mix until well combined, about 2 minutes.
3. Add the egg and vanilla extract and mix until fluffy and lighter in color, about 1 minute.
4. Add the flour, cornstarch, baking soda, and salt. Mix on low until just combined, about 30 seconds.
5. Add the M&M's and mix on low until evenly distributed throughout the dough.
6. Use a large (4-tablespoon/2-ounce) cookie scoop to scoop the dough into balls. Place up to five dough balls onto each baking sheet, spaced equally apart.
7. Bake for 9 to 11 minutes, until the edges are just set. Let the cookies cool on the baking sheets for 5 minutes and then transfer to a cooling rack to cool completely.

NOTE

You can use Reese's Pieces or chocolate chips instead of the M&M's if you wish.

OATMEAL RAISIN COOKIES

I've never met a human who doesn't like a good cookie. I've met plenty of humans who don't like oatmeal raisin cookies, but I'm here to tell you that they've probably just never had a good oatmeal raisin cookie. Oatmeal raisin cookies get a lot of hate, and if they're the dry, crusty cookies in your grandma's pantry, then that's probably warranted. But all that hate will quickly disappear when you try this recipe. These oatmeal raisin cookies are unbelievably soft (and stay soft thanks to the oats), and the raisins add such a delightful, sweet bite. Plus, they're rolled in cinnamon sugar, making them snickerdoodle-esque, with the perfect amount of cinnamon flavor. They're the best oatmeal raisin cookies you'll ever try.

MAKES 7 LARGE COOKIES

½ cup (113 g) salted butter, softened

½ cup (108 g) brown sugar

¼ cup (50 g) plus 1 tablespoon granulated sugar, divided

1 large egg plus 1 large egg yolk, room temperature

1 teaspoon vanilla extract

1 cup (130 g) all-purpose flour

1 cup (90 g) rolled oats

¾ teaspoon Diamond Crystal kosher salt

½ teaspoon baking soda

½ cup (75 g) raisins (see Note)

1 teaspoon ground cinnamon

1. Preheat the oven to 350°F (180°C). Line two baking sheets with parchment paper.
2. Place the butter, brown sugar, and ¼ cup (50 g) granulated sugar in a large bowl. Use a stand mixer or hand mixer to mix until combined, about 3 minutes.
3. Add the egg, egg yolk, and vanilla extract. Mix until combined, about 1 minute.
4. Add the flour, rolled oats, salt, and baking soda. Mix until just combined, about 30 seconds.
5. Add the raisins and mix on low, until evenly distributed throughout the dough.
6. Mix the remaining tablespoon of granulated sugar and the cinnamon in a small bowl.
7. Use a large (4-tablespoon/2-ounce) cookie scoop to scoop the dough into balls. Roll each dough ball in the palms of your hands until smooth and then drop it into the cinnamon sugar and roll to coat.
8. Place up to four dough balls onto each baking sheet, spaced equally apart. Bake for 8 to 10 minutes, until the edges are just starting to set. The middles of the cookies may still look soft, but as they cool, they will continue to cook.
9. Let the cookies cool on the baking sheets for 10 minutes and then transfer to a cooling rack to cool completely.

NOTE

OK, OK, if you hate raisins and really can't deal with them, you can substitute another dried fruit. Dried cranberries, blueberries, or cherries would all be delightful!

DOUBLE CHOCOLATE COOKIES

Double chocolate cookies, because when has single chocolate been enough? To be honest with you, I'm not usually a fan of double chocolate cookies. They are typically a little too rich for me, even though I am a chocolate lover. But the milk chocolate chunks in these cookies create the perfect balance for me. The sweet milk chocolate cuts through the rich cocoa powder. If you love a chocolate cookie that is as dark and rich as can be, use Dutch-process cocoa powder and dark chocolate chunks.

MAKES 9 LARGE COOKIES

½ cup (113 g) salted butter, softened

½ cup (108 g) brown sugar

½ cup (100 g) granulated sugar

1 large egg, room temperature

2 teaspoons vanilla extract

1 cup (130 g) all-purpose flour

½ cup (42 g) cocoa powder

1 teaspoon Diamond Crystal kosher salt

½ teaspoon baking soda

1½ cups (255 g) milk, semisweet, or dark chocolate chunks, plus extra for topping

Flaky salt, for topping, optional

1. Preheat the oven to 350°F (180°C). Line two baking sheets with parchment paper.
2. Place the butter, brown sugar, and granulated sugar in a large bowl. Use a stand mixer or hand mixer to mix until combined, about 2 minutes.
3. Add the egg and vanilla extract. Mix until combined and fluffy, about 1 minute.
4. Add the flour, cocoa powder, kosher salt, and baking soda. Mix on low just until no streaks of flour remain, about 30 seconds.
5. Add the chocolate chunks. Mix on low to distribute evenly throughout the dough.
6. Use a large (4-tablespoon/2-ounce) cookie scoop to scoop the dough into balls. Place up to five balls onto each baking sheet, spaced equally apart. Top each dough ball with a chocolate chunk, gently pressing the chunks into the dough.
7. Bake for 9 to 11 minutes, until the edges are just starting to set. Top each cookie with a pinch of flaky salt, if desired. Let the cookies cool on the baking sheets for 10 minutes and then transfer to a cooling rack to cool completely.

SOFT GINGERBREAD COOKIES

This recipe stems from a feud between my parents. When they were dating, they realized they both had a gingerbread cookie recipe they were proud of, so the only way to determine a winner was to have a competition. They each made their recipe, tried each other's cookies, and had others judge, too. And . . . my dad won in a landslide. Ever since then, these cookies have been a staple in my family. Throughout my childhood, we made them constantly and always had a stash in the freezer so we could bake them whenever we wanted. I've adjusted the recipe ever so slightly from the original (sorry, Dad), but I think these are even better.

MAKES 10 LARGE COOKIES

1 cup (200 g) granulated sugar, divided

¾ cup (170 g) salted butter, softened

¼ cup (54 g) brown sugar

1 large egg, room temperature

¼ cup (85 g) molasses

2 cups (260 g) all-purpose flour

1 teaspoon baking soda

1 teaspoon ground cinnamon

1 teaspoon ground ginger

1 teaspoon Diamond Crystal kosher salt

1. Preheat the oven to 350°F (180°C). Line two baking sheets with parchment paper.
2. Place ¾ cup (150 g) granulated sugar along with the butter and brown sugar in a large bowl. Use a stand mixer or hand mixer to mix until combined, about 3 minutes.
3. Add the egg and molasses and mix until combined, about 1 minute.
4. Add the flour, baking soda, cinnamon, ginger, and salt. Mix on low to combine, about 1 minute.
5. Place the remaining ¼ cup (50 g) granulated sugar in a shallow bowl.
6. Use a large (4-tablespoon/2-ounce) cookie scoop to scoop the dough into balls. Roll each ball in the palms of your hands until smooth then drop into the sugar and roll to coat. Place up to five dough balls onto each baking sheet, spaced equally apart.
7. Bake for 8 to 11 minutes, until the edges are just starting to set. Let the cookies cool on the baking sheets for 10 minutes and then transfer to a cooling rack to cool completely.

WHITE CHOCOLATE MACADAMIA NUT COOKIES

Macadamia nuts have such a distinctive flavor profile. They've got a creamy, buttery taste (thanks to their high fat content), so it's no wonder they're good in cookies. I'm a firm believer that macadamia nut cookies should be soft, not crunchy or dry, and these cookies are just that. The coconut flakes are optional, but they give these cookies a tropical feel that I can't get enough of. Add a bit of lime zest on top and close your eyes, and you might just be in paradise!

MAKES 8 LARGE COOKIES

½ cup (113 g) salted butter, softened

½ cup (108 g) brown sugar

⅓ cup (66 g) granulated sugar

1 large egg, room temperature

1 teaspoon vanilla extract

1⅓ cups (173 g) all-purpose flour

½ teaspoon baking powder

½ teaspoon Diamond Crystal kosher salt

½ cup (85 g) white chocolate chips

½ cup (75 g) unsalted macadamia nuts, chopped

½ cup (26 g) unsweetened coconut flakes, optional

1. Preheat the oven to 350°F (180°C). Line two baking sheets with parchment paper.
2. Heat a medium pan over medium heat. Cut the butter in half and then cut each half into ½-inch (1 cm) cubes. Place half of the cubes in a large bowl. Add the other half to the pan and stir until melted, about 2 minutes. Keep stirring until the butter starts to bubble and then foam, about 2 minutes. After the foam subsides, you'll see brown flecks on the bottom of the pan, and the butter will smell very nutty. Pour the brown butter into the bowl with the remaining butter and stir until the cubes of butter melt.
3. Set aside for 10 minutes, or until the butter is warm and liquid but not hot to the touch. Add the brown sugar and granulated sugar and use a stand or hand mixer to mix until combined.
4. Add the egg and vanilla extract and mix until combined, about 1 minute.
5. Add the flour, baking powder, and salt and mix on low until just combined, about 30 seconds.
6. Add the white chocolate chips, macadamia nuts, and coconut flakes, if using. Mix until evenly distributed throughout the dough.
7. Use a large (4-tablespoon/2-ounce) cookie scoop to scoop the dough into balls. Place up to four balls onto each baking sheet, spaced equally apart.
8. Bake for 8 to 10 minutes, until the edges are just set. The middles will still look very soft, but the cookies will continue to cook as they cool.
9. Let the cookies cool on the baking sheet for 10 minutes and then transfer to a cooling rack to cool completely.

SUGAR COOKIES

These cookies were my grandma's specialty. Any day we walked into her house, we knew she'd have some on hand. They were usually stored in the freezer, where she kept them after making a giant batch. We were much too impatient to wait for them to fully thaw, so I'm used to eating these cookies cold, and I actually prefer them that way. They are soft and have the perfect balance of flavor from the almond and vanilla extracts. They don't spread much when they bake, so they're perfect to cut out into whatever shape you want. You can store them at room temperature, but I'd highly recommend Grandma Loma's method: Keep them chilled in the fridge (or freezer)!

MAKES 20 LARGE COOKIES

Sugar Cookies

1 cup (200 g) granulated sugar

½ cup (113 g) salted butter, softened

½ cup (120 ml) buttermilk, room temperature (see Note)

1 large egg, room temperature

½ teaspoon vanilla extract

½ teaspoon almond extract

3½ cups (455 g) all-purpose flour, plus extra if needed and for dusting

½ teaspoon baking soda

½ teaspoon Diamond Crystal kosher salt

Vanilla Buttercream Frosting

½ cup (113 g) salted butter, softened

2 cups (227 g) powdered sugar

1 tablespoon milk

1 teaspoon vanilla extract

Food coloring, optional

1. Preheat the oven to 325°F (165°C). Line two baking sheets with parchment paper.
2. Make the cookies: Place the sugar and butter in a large bowl. Use a stand mixer or hand mixer to mix until fluffy and lighter in color, about 3 minutes.
3. Add the buttermilk, egg, vanilla extract, and almond extract. Mix until well combined, about 2 minutes.
4. Add the flour, baking soda, and salt. Mix on low until just combined, about 30 seconds. The dough should be very soft but not super sticky. If it is sticky, add more flour, 2 tablespoons at a time, mixing until just combined between each addition, until the dough is no longer sticky.
5. Transfer the dough to a lightly floured counter. Use a rolling pin to roll out the dough ¼ inch (6 mm) thick. Use a cookie cutter or a round glass cup to cut out the dough. Reroll and cut the remaining dough until all the dough is used.
6. Carefully transfer up to 8 large cookies onto each baking sheet, spaced at least 1 inch (2.5 cm) apart.
7. Bake for 10 to 12 minutes, until the middles are just set. If you touch them lightly, they should spring back. Let the cookies cool on the baking sheets for 10 minutes and then transfer to a cooling rack to cool completely.
8. Once the baking sheets are cool to the touch, repeat steps 6 and 7 to bake any remaining dough.

NOTE

If you don't have buttermilk, add 1 teaspoon apple cider vinegar to ½ cup (120 ml) milk.

9. Meanwhile, make the frosting: Place the butter in a large bowl. Use a stand mixer or hand mixer to mix for 1 minute. Add the powdered sugar, milk, and vanilla extract. Mix until well combined and smooth, about 2 minutes. Add the food coloring, if using, and mix until well combined, about 1 minute.

10. When the cookies are completely cool, use a small offset spatula to spread the frosting on each cookie in an even layer.

BROWNIE COOKIES

Fudgy versus cakey brownies has been one of the great debates of my marriage. I am firmly in the fudgy category, while my husband, Connor, is team cakey all day. Luckily, our marriage is built on more than just brownies, so this hasn't torn us apart. And lucky for me, I am the author of this book, so this recipe results in fudgy brownie cookies (although I included a Note at the bottom of the page about how to make them cakier—love you, Connor). These cookies are exactly what they sound like: brownies in cookie form. They're rich and chocolatey, and just like with normal brownies, the eggs are whipped until they get glossy and frothy, which creates a beautiful crinkle top.

MAKES 36 MEDIUM COOKIES

1 cup (170 g) semisweet chocolate chips
½ cup (113 g) salted butter
½ cup (108 g) brown sugar
½ cup (100 g) granulated sugar
3 large eggs, room temperature
1 teaspoon vanilla extract
1½ cups (195 g) all-purpose flour
¼ cup (21 g) cocoa powder
½ teaspoon baking powder
½ teaspoon Diamond Crystal kosher salt

1. Preheat the oven to 350°F (180°C). Line two baking sheets with parchment paper.
2. Heat a large pan over medium heat. Add the chocolate chips and butter. Stir until the butter and chocolate melt, about 3 minutes, and then turn off the heat and set aside to cool.
3. Place the brown sugar, granulated sugar, and eggs in a large bowl. Use a hand mixer or stand mixer to mix until the sugar mostly dissolves and the mixture is glossy and lighter in color, about 3 minutes.
4. Pour the chocolate into the bowl with the sugar and eggs. Add the vanilla extract and mix until combined, about 30 seconds.
5. Add the flour, cocoa powder, baking powder, and salt. Mix on low just until no streaks of flour remain, about 30 seconds.
6. Use a medium (2-tablespoon/1-ounce) cookie scoop to scoop the dough into balls.
7. Place up to six dough balls onto each baking sheet, spaced equally apart. Bake for 9 to 12 minutes, until the tops of the cookies are crinkly and the edges are just starting to set. Let the cookies cool on the baking sheets for 10 minutes and then transfer to a cooling rack to cool completely.
8. Once the baking sheets are cool to the touch, repeat step 7 to bake the remaining dough.

NOTE

For cakier brownie cookies, add 2 additional tablespoons of all-purpose flour to the dough and add 1 or 2 minutes to the bake time.

BIRTHDAY CAKE COOKIES

My four-year-old told me that it's impossible to be sad with a birthday cake cookie in hand, and honestly, she's not wrong. Sprinkles are just inherently happy. These cookies have a soft sugar-cookie base packed with plenty of sprinkles, and they're topped with a streusel that is also stuffed with sprinkles. If you're celebrating something other than a birthday, switch out the rainbow sprinkles to match the holiday! Valentine's Day, Christmas, Halloween—this cookie is your go-to for any celebration.

MAKES 7 LARGE COOKIES

Birthday Cake Cookies

⅔ cup (133 g) granulated sugar

½ cup (113 g) salted butter, softened

⅓ cup (72 g) brown sugar

1 large egg, room temperature

1 teaspoon vanilla extract

1½ cups (195 g) all-purpose flour

1 teaspoon Diamond Crystal kosher salt

½ teaspoon baking powder

½ teaspoon baking soda

¼ cup (50 g) rainbow sprinkles

Crumble (see Note)

½ cup (65 g) all-purpose flour

¼ cup (56 g) salted butter, softened

¼ cup (50 g) granulated sugar

1 tablespoon rainbow sprinkles

½ teaspoon vanilla extract

Pinch of Diamond Crystal kosher salt

1. Preheat the oven to 350°F (180°C). Line two baking sheets with parchment paper.
2. Make the cookies: Place the granulated sugar, butter, and brown sugar in a large bowl. Use a stand mixer or hand mixer to mix until lighter in color, about 3 minutes.
3. Add the egg and vanilla extract. Mix until well combined and slightly fluffy, about 2 minutes.
4. Add the flour, salt, baking powder, and baking soda. Mix on low until no streaks of flour remain, about 30 seconds. Add the sprinkles and mix on low until just distributed throughout the dough.
5. Make the crumble: Place the flour, butter, sugar, sprinkles, vanilla extract, and salt in a medium bowl. Use a hand mixer or rubber spatula to mix until no streaks of flour remain, about 1 minute. The mixture should hold together when squeezed into a ball but crumble if you run your fingers through it.
6. Use a large (4-tablespoon/2-ounce) cookie scoop to scoop the dough into balls. Use the back of the cookie scoop (or the back of a spoon) to make a divot in the top of each cookie, about ½ inch (1 cm) deep. Place about 1 tablespoon of the crumble in each divot.
7. Place up to four dough balls onto each baking sheet, spaced equally apart. Bake for 9 to 11 minutes, until the edges are just starting to set. Let the cookies cool on the baking sheet for 10 minutes and then transfer to a cooling rack to cool completely.

NOTE

If you don't want the crumble on top, you can just omit it entirely! You may need to bake the cookies for 1 or 2 minutes less because they won't have the extra weight on top.

SHORTBREAD

There's something so special about the simplicity of shortbread—it's what makes it so good. No frosting, no mix-ins, just a flaky, buttery cookie. The higher ratio of butter to sugar is what gives us a tender, flaky crumb that isn't too sweet. And the turbinado sugar on the outside lends a lovely crunch. I recommend using a high-quality butter for all of my cookies, but these are ones where you'll really be able to tell the difference. This is a roll-and-slice shortbread, but if you're interested in shortbread bars, see my Ted Lasso *Shortbread Cookies on page 179.*

MAKES ABOUT 30 MEDIUM COOKIES

1 cup (227 g) salted butter, cold
½ cup (100 g) granulated sugar
2 large egg yolks, cold
1 teaspoon vanilla extract
3 cups (390 g) all-purpose flour
½ teaspoon Diamond Crystal kosher salt
2 to 3 tablespoons cold water
¼ cup (45 g) turbinado sugar, optional (see Note)

1. Cut the butter into 1-inch (2.5 cm) cubes. Place the butter and sugar in a large bowl. Use a stand mixer or hand mixer to mix until combined, about 3 minutes.
2. Add the egg yolks and vanilla extract and mix until combined and creamy, about 2 minutes.
3. Add the flour and salt. Mix until just combined. The dough will be very crumbly and shaggy. With the mixer on low, add the cold water a tablespoon at a time and mix until a soft dough forms, about 1 minute.
4. Transfer the dough to a large piece of plastic wrap. Use your hands to shape the dough into a log about 10 inches (25 cm) long and 2 inches (5 cm) wide. Wrap the dough with the plastic wrap and transfer to the fridge to chill for 1 hour.
5. Preheat the oven to 350°F (180°C). Line two baking sheets with parchment paper.
6. Remove the dough from the plastic wrap. If you're using the turbinado sugar, pour it onto a small baking sheet and roll the dough in the sugar, pressing down to help the sugar stick.
7. Use a sharp knife to cut the log into ¼-inch (6 mm) slices.
8. Place up to twelve slices onto each baking sheet, spaced equally apart. Bake for 7 to 9 minutes, until the centers no longer look doughy. Let the cookies cool for 10 minutes on the baking sheet and then transfer to a cooling rack to cool completely.
9. Repeat step 8 to bake the remaining dough.

NOTE

If you can't find turbinado sugar, you can roll the log in granulated sugar or just not roll it in anything.

UNEXPECTED FLAVORS

Take everything you know about the classic cookie flavors in The Classics chapter (page 77) and throw it out the window. I love pushing the bounds of what a cookie can be. I live for turning obscure ingredients into a cookie that just works, and that's exactly what this chapter achieves. Look in your pantry and fridge, find all the things you thought you'd never put in a cookie (think cheddar cheese on page 117, chili crisp on page 106, and preserved lemon on page 105), and you're ready to start baking! From Miso Toffee Snickerdoodles (page 100) to Hot Honey Cookies (page 118), these will be the most unique cookies you'll ever make.

MISO TOFFEE SNICKERDOODLES

Miso is such a powerful little ingredient. It's a traditional Japanese seasoning that comes in the form of a thick paste and is made by combining soybeans, salt, and koji (a type of fungus cultivated on rice, barley, or other grains). The mixture is left to ferment for months or even years and is used in sauces, spreads, miso soup, and so much more. And it also happens to be incredible in desserts. Miso is packed with savory umami flavor, and when it's added to sweets like cookies, its beautiful, subtle saltiness provides a perfect balance. For these cookies, we're taking miso dough, adding lots of toffee bits, and then rolling each dough ball in cinnamon sugar. This unexpected take on a snickerdoodle will have you speechless at the beautiful dance between salty and sweet.

MAKES 8 LARGE COOKIES

Toffee

½ cup (100 g) granulated sugar

2 tablespoons unsalted butter

2 tablespoons water

Pinch of Diamond Crystal kosher salt

Miso Snickerdoodles

½ cup (113 g) salted butter, softened

½ cup (108 g) brown sugar

¼ cup (50 g) plus 2 tablespoons granulated sugar, divided

1 large egg, room temperature

2 tablespoons white miso paste (see Note)

1 teaspoon vanilla extract

1½ cups (195 g) all-purpose flour

1½ teaspoons cornstarch

½ teaspoon baking soda

½ teaspoon Diamond Crystal kosher salt

1½ teaspoons ground cinnamon

NOTE

Any type of miso will work! White miso has the subtlest flavor. For a stronger flavor, use red miso.

1. Make the toffee: Line a baking sheet with parchment paper. Heat a medium heavy-bottomed pot over medium-low heat. Add the granulated sugar, butter, water, and salt. Stir to combine with a wooden spoon.
2. Continue to gently stir until the butter melts, about 3 minutes, and then stop actively stirring. The mixture will start to bubble. Stir occasionally, about once every 2 minutes, and let boil until the mixture turns a medium-brown color and reaches 295°F to 305°F (146°C to 151°C) on a candy thermometer, 10 to 14 minutes.
3. Carefully pour the hot mixture onto the prepared baking sheet and use the back of your spoon to spread it into a thin, even layer. Set aside and let cool completely before using the back of a spoon to break it into small pieces.
4. Preheat the oven to 350°F (180°C). Line two baking sheets with parchment paper.
5. Make the cookies: Place the butter, the brown sugar, and ¼ cup (50 g) granulated sugar in a large bowl. Use a stand mixer or hand mixer to mix until well combined, about 3 minutes.
6. Add the egg, miso paste, and vanilla extract. Mix until combined, about 2 minutes.
7. Add the flour, cornstarch, baking soda, and salt. Mix on low until just combined, about 30 seconds.

recipe continues...

8. Add 1 cup (156 g) of the toffee bits. Mix on low until evenly distributed throughout the dough.
9. Mix the remaining 2 tablespoons granulated sugar and the cinnamon in a small bowl.
10. Use a large (4-tablespoon/2-ounce) cookie scoop to scoop the dough into balls. Roll each dough ball in the palms of your hands until smooth and then drop it into the cinnamon sugar and roll to coat.
11. Place up to four dough balls onto each baking sheet, spaced equally apart. Bake for 9 to 12 minutes, until the edges are just set.
12. Let the cookies cool on the baking sheets for 10 minutes and then transfer to a cooling rack to cool completely.

PRESERVED LEMON AND HONEY COOKIES

Preserved lemons are such an intriguing food. Originating in North African and Middle Eastern cooking, they are essentially a type of pickle. Fresh lemons are packed into a jar with a brine of lemon juice and salt and then are left to ferment at room temperature for several weeks. The fermentation process tempers the bitterness and acidity of the lemons and accentuates the lemon flavor. Meanwhile, the brine creates a salty, umami kick. Enter these cookies: strong lemon flavor with a slight umami tang, balanced out by sweet honey and then coated in sesame seeds for a nutty finish. These cookies are thin and chewy, and they definitely earn their place in this chapter of unexpected flavors.

MAKES 20 MEDIUM COOKIES

1 preserved lemon or zest of 3 lemons (about 3 tablespoons) (see Note)

½ cup (113 g) salted butter, softened

¼ cup (84 g) honey

⅓ cup (72 g) brown sugar

⅓ cup (66 g) granulated sugar

1 large egg, room temperature

1 teaspoon vanilla extract

1⅓ cups (173 g) all-purpose flour

½ teaspoon baking soda

½ teaspoon Diamond Crystal kosher salt

½ cup (70 g) toasted sesame seeds

NOTE

If you can't find preserved lemons and don't want to make your own, you can use lemon zest instead. The lemon flavor won't be quite as strong, and you'll be missing the slight salty kick, but they will still be lovely lemon cookies!

1. Preheat the oven to 350°F (180°C). Line two baking sheets with parchment paper.
2. Rinse the preserved lemon thoroughly with water and then remove the flesh. Finely chop the rind.
3. Place the butter and honey in a large bowl. Use a hand mixer or stand mixer to mix until combined, about 1 minute. Add the brown sugar and granulated sugar and mix until lighter in color, about 2 minutes.
4. Add the preserved lemon, egg, and vanilla extract. Mix until combined, about 1 minute.
5. Add the flour, baking soda, and salt. Mix on low until the flour is just combined, about 30 seconds. Cover the bowl and transfer to the fridge to chill for at least 30 minutes.
6. Place the sesame seeds in a shallow bowl.
7. Use a medium (2-tablespoon/1-ounce) cookie scoop to scoop the dough into balls. Drop each dough ball into the sesame seeds and roll to coat.
8. Place up to six dough balls onto each baking sheet, spaced equally apart. Bake for 10 to 12 minutes, until the edges are golden brown. Let the cookies cool on the baking sheets for 5 minutes and then transfer to a cooling rack to cool completely.
9. Once the baking sheets are cool to the touch, repeat step 8 to bake the remaining dough.

CHILI CRISP COOKIES

I know what you're thinking, and yes, you read that right: chili crisp cookies. The same chili crisp that you put on your ramen and your eggs to spice them up is going in these cookies. And before you think I've gone too crazy, do remember that this chapter is called "Unexpected Flavors"—and what's more unexpected than this? I'm not completely insane, though—I didn't add the chili crisp directly into the dough. Otherwise, every bite would be a fiery, garlicky burst. Instead, I made a chili crisp brittle that's very sweet and has a strong, spicy aftertaste (with a subtle garlic flavor). It gets broken up into small pieces and then added to the dough with coconut, toasted sesame seeds, and caramelized white chocolate. The chili crisp is contained to the brittle, adding small pockets of strong spiciness that are balanced out beautifully by all the other mix-ins. It will definitely be the craziest cookie you ever bake, but you'll be shocked to find yourself making it over and over.

MAKES 16 MEDIUM COOKIES

Caramelized White Chocolate

1 cup (170 g) white chocolate chips or chunks

Chili Crisp Brittle

¼ cup (50 g) granulated sugar

1 tablespoon salted butter

1 tablespoon water

1 teaspoon chili crisp (see Note 1)

¼ teaspoon baking soda

⅛ teaspoon Diamond Crystal kosher salt

Coconut and Sesame Cookies

½ cup (113 g) salted butter, softened

½ cup (100 g) granulated sugar

¼ cup (54 g) brown sugar

1 large egg, room temperature

1 teaspoon vanilla extract

1¼ cups (162 g) all-purpose flour

½ teaspoon Diamond Crystal kosher salt

½ teaspoon baking soda

¾ cup (45 g) unsweetened shredded coconut

2 tablespoons toasted sesame seeds

1. Make the caramelized white chocolate: Preheat the oven to 250°F (120°C). Line a baking sheet with parchment paper.
2. Place the white chocolate on the baking sheet. Bake for 40 to 60 minutes, until the chocolate is deeply golden, using an offset spatula to stir and smooth it out every 10 minutes. Set aside to cool and then chop into small chunks (see Note 2).
3. Make the brittle: Line a baking sheet with parchment paper. Heat the sugar, butter, and water in a medium pot over medium heat. Stir continually until the butter melts, about 2 minutes. When the mixture starts to bubble, about 1 more minute, stop actively stirring.
4. Continue to cook, swirling the pot every minute to gently stir, until the sugar starts to turn light brown, 3 to 5 minutes. Turn off the heat. Add the chili crisp, stirring until combined, and then quickly stir in the baking soda and salt.
5. Carefully pour the hot mixture onto the baking sheet. Use the back of a spoon to spread the brittle into a thin layer. Set aside to cool completely and then use the back of a spoon to break it into smaller chunks.
6. Make the cookies: Preheat the oven to 350°F (180°C). Line two baking sheets with parchment paper.
7. Place the butter, granulated sugar, and brown sugar in a large bowl. Use a stand mixer or hand mixer to mix until combined, about 2 minutes.

8. Add the egg and vanilla extract and mix until fluffy and lighter in color, about 1 minute. Add the flour, salt, and baking soda. Mix on low just until the flour is combined, about 30 seconds.
9. Add the coconut and sesame seeds. Reserve a handful of the brittle and chocolate (for topping) and then add the remaining brittle and chocolate to the dough. Mix on low, until the mix-ins are evenly distributed throughout the dough.
10. Use a medium (2-tablespoon/1-ounce) cookie scoop to scoop the dough into balls. Top each dough ball with the reserved chunks of chili crisp brittle and chocolate, gently pressing them into the dough. Place up to eight dough balls onto each baking sheet, spaced equally apart.
11. Bake for 8 to 10 minutes, until the edges start to brown. Let the cookies cool on the baking sheets for 10 minutes and then transfer to a cooling rack to cool completely.

NOTES

1. Any brand of chili crisp will work. I've used Lao Gan Ma, Momofuku, and Fly By Jing, and each was great. Whatever brand you use, make sure you're getting as much of the crisp and as little of the oil as possible.

2. The white chocolate may become very chunky in the caramelizing process. This is totally fine. If the chocolate is still chunky when it reaches a golden color, transfer it to a food processor and blend until smooth, about 2 minutes. Then, pour it onto a piece of parchment paper, smooth it out with an offset spatula, and set aside to cool.

HALVA BLACK SESAME COOKIES

Halva is a fudge-like candy made of tahini that originated in the Middle East. It has a rich, slightly bitter sweetness from the sesame seeds, and its dense-yet-crumbly texture will melt in your mouth. When added to cookies, the halva melts into the dough, creating a soft, nutty bite. The sweet tahini candy pairs perfectly with the even nuttier black sesame seeds in this recipe. These cookies are no doubt heavy on the sesame flavor, but it works so well.

MAKES 22 MEDIUM COOKIES

¾ cup (170 g) salted butter, softened

¾ cup (162 g) brown sugar

⅓ cup (66 g) granulated sugar

1 large egg plus 1 large egg yolk, room temperature

1 teaspoon vanilla extract

1¾ cups (227 g) all-purpose flour

1 teaspoon baking powder

1 teaspoon Diamond Crystal kosher salt

½ teaspoon baking soda

¼ cup (35 g) black sesame seeds

½ cup (116 g) halva, divided

1. Preheat the oven to 350°F (180°C). Line two baking sheets with parchment paper.
2. Place the butter, brown sugar, and granulated sugar in a large bowl. Use a stand mixer or hand mixer to mix until combined, about 2 minutes.
3. Add the egg, egg yolk, and vanilla extract. Mix until combined and fluffy, about 1 minute.
4. Add the flour, baking powder, salt, and baking soda. Mix on low until just combined, about 30 seconds.
5. Add the sesame seeds. Break ¼ cup (58 g) of the halva into smaller chunks, each about ½ inch (1 cm) wide, and add to the mixture. Mix on low until just combined .
6. Use a medium (2-tablespoon/1-ounce) cookie scoop to scoop the dough into balls. Place a small chunk (about ½ teaspoon) of the remaining halva on top of each dough ball, pressing down gently to adhere.
7. Place up to six dough balls onto each baking sheet, spaced equally apart.
8. Bake for 8 to 10 minutes, until the edges are just starting to brown. Let the cookies cool on the baking sheets for 10 minutes and then transfer to a cooling rack to cool completely.
9. Repeat steps 7 and 8 to bake the remaining dough.

SWIRLED MALTED COOKIES

When you hear "malt," you may think of a milkshake or malt balls, but probably not cookies (until now!). Or maybe you think of Ovaltine—the chocolate malt powder added to milk to make a cozy drink. Malted milk is made from malted barley and evaporated milk, and it has a rich, nutty flavor with hints of caramel. For these cookies, a simple dough is divided in half—one half gets malted milk, and the other half gets homemade Ovaltine (malted milk plus cocoa powder). Then, the dough is swirled together to create the perfect balance of flavors, with the malt flavor shining throughout.

MAKES 7 LARGE COOKIES

½ cup (113 g) salted butter, softened

⅓ cup (72 g) brown sugar

⅓ cup (66 g) granulated sugar

1 large egg, room temperature

1 teaspoon vanilla extract

1¼ cups (162 g) all-purpose flour

1 teaspoon Diamond Crystal kosher salt

½ teaspoon baking powder

3 tablespoons malted milk, divided

1 tablespoon cocoa powder

1. Preheat the oven to 350°F (180°C). Line two baking sheets with parchment paper.
2. Place the butter, brown sugar, and granulated sugar in a large bowl. Use a stand mixer or hand mixer to mix until combined, about 2 minutes.
3. Add the egg and vanilla extract and mix until fluffy and lighter in color, about 1 minute.
4. Add the flour, salt, and baking powder. Mix on low just until the flour is combined.
5. Divide the dough in half; each half should weigh about 8 ounces (227 g). Leave half of the dough in the large bowl and place the other half in a medium bowl. Add 2 tablespoons malted milk to the dough in the large bowl. Mix until just combined.
6. Add the remaining 1 tablespoon malted milk and the cocoa powder (see Note) to the dough in the medium bowl. Use a rubber spatula to mix until just combined.
7. Using a large (4-tablespoon/2-ounce) cookie scoop, scoop about 1 tablespoon of one dough and then 1 tablespoon of the other dough, alternating back and forth until the cookie scoop is full. This will create a swirled look. Place up to four dough balls onto each baking sheet, spaced equally apart.
8. Bake for 10 to 12 minutes, until the edges are just set. Let the cookies cool on the baking sheets for 10 minutes and then transfer to a cooling rack to cool completely.

NOTE

If you have Ovaltine on hand, you can just use 2 tablespoons Ovaltine for the chocolate half of the dough instead of the malted milk and cocoa powder.

RYE, PISTACHIO, AND SESAME CCC

There are a lot of things that make these cookies special, but rye flour really takes them to the next level. Rye flour is milled from rye kernels, aka rye berries. It has a vibrant, earthy flavor that really sets it apart from your typical wheat flour, and it pairs perfectly with the pistachios and sesame seeds. The flavor of this cookie is balanced by pools of dark chocolate throughout and a generous pinch of flaky salt on top.

MAKES 9 LARGE COOKIES

½ cup (113 g) salted butter, softened

½ cup (108 g) brown sugar

⅓ cup (66 g) granulated sugar

1 large egg plus 1 large egg yolk, room temperature

1 teaspoon vanilla extract

1⅓ cups (150 g) rye flour (see Note 1)

½ teaspoon baking soda

½ teaspoon Diamond Crystal kosher salt

¼ teaspoon baking powder

½ cup (85 g) dark chocolate chunks, plus extra for topping

½ cup (60 g) shelled pistachios, chopped (see Note 2)

2 tablespoons sesame seeds

Flaky salt, for topping

1. Preheat the oven to 350°F (180°C). Line two baking sheets with parchment paper.
2. Place the butter, brown sugar, and granulated sugar in a bowl. Use a stand mixer or hand mixer to mix until fully combined, about 2 minutes.
3. Add the egg, egg yolk, and vanilla extract and mix until fully combined, about 1 minute.
4. Add the flour, baking soda, kosher salt, and baking powder. Mix until just combined, about 30 seconds.
5. Add the chocolate chunks and pistachios and mix on low until evenly distributed through the dough.
6. Use a large (4-tablespoon/2-ounce) cookie scoop to scoop the dough into balls. Top each dough ball with a chunk of chocolate, gently pressing the chunks into the dough.
7. Place the sesame seeds in a shallow bowl and then gently press the top of each dough ball into the seeds (see Note 3).
8. Place up to five dough balls onto each baking sheet, spaced equally apart.
9. Bake for 8 to 10 minutes, until the edges are just set. Top each cookie with a pinch of flaky salt. Let the cookies cool on the baking sheets for 5 minutes and then transfer to a cooling rack to cool completely.

NOTES

1. Rye flour comes in three different varieties: light, medium, and dark. For these cookies, use light (also called white) or medium rye flour. If you can't find rye flour, substitute 1¼ cups (162 g) all-purpose flour instead.

2. If pistachios are a no-go, feel free to substitute with hazelnuts.

3. For these cookies to look their best, don't cover the entire surface in sesame seeds. After you place the chocolate chunk on top, dip a few parts of the surrounding surface in sesame seeds. This patchwork approach makes the cookies look much prettier.

BLOOD ORANGE, CARDAMOM, AND PISTACHIO COOKIES

There are certain recipes that take test after test after test to get just right. These cookies caused me a headache, but we finally got there. I originally wanted them to be upside-down blood orange cookies, but no matter what I tried, I couldn't prevent the cookies from becoming soggy from the slices of orange on the bottoms (though they looked stunning). Finally, I pivoted, and I honestly like where these landed ten times more! Olive oil gives these cookies a zesty punch while blood orange provides a bright citrus flavor, and then both of those flavors are evened out by the softness of the cardamom and the fattiness of the pistachios. Each cookie is finished with a dip in blood orange icing that ties it all together, and the result is the most delightful cookie: fresh and bright and warm.

MAKES 9 LARGE COOKIES

Cardamom and Pistachio Cookies

¼ cup (50 g) granulated sugar

Zest of ½ blood orange (about 1 tablespoon)

¾ cup (162 g) brown sugar

½ cup (120 ml) olive oil

1 large egg plus 1 large egg yolk, room temperature

1 teaspoon vanilla extract

1½ cups (195 g) all-purpose flour

1 teaspoon ground cardamom

1 teaspoon Diamond Crystal kosher salt

½ teaspoon baking powder

½ teaspoon baking soda

½ cup (60 g) shelled pistachios, chopped, plus extra for topping

Blood Orange Icing

1 cup (113 g) powdered sugar

Juice of ½ blood orange (2 to 3 tablespoons; see Note)

1. Preheat the oven to 350°F (180°C). Line two baking sheets with parchment paper.
2. Place the granulated sugar and orange zest in a large bowl. Use your fingers to rub the orange zest into the sugar, releasing the orange oil.
3. Add the brown sugar and olive oil. Use a stand mixer or hand mixer to mix until combined. Mix in the egg, egg yolk, and vanilla extract.
4. Add the flour, cardamom, salt, baking powder, and baking soda. Mix on low just until no streaks of flour remain, about 30 seconds. Add the pistachios and mix on low until evenly distributed through the dough.
5. Use a large (4-tablespoon/2-ounce) cookie scoop to scoop the dough into balls. Use your hands to roll each one into a smooth ball.
6. Place up to five dough balls onto each baking sheet, spaced equally apart. Bake for 10 to 12 minutes, until the edges are just set. Let the cookies cool on the baking sheets for 10 minutes and then transfer to a cooling rack to cool.
7. Meanwhile, make the icing: Whisk the powdered sugar and 2 tablespoons of orange juice in a small bowl until smooth. If the icing is thick and hard to stir, add the additional tablespoon of juice. The glaze should be smooth and just thick enough to coat the back of a spoon.

8. When the cookies are completely cool, dip the top half of each cookie in the icing and then transfer back to the cooling rack to allow any excess icing to drip off. Top the icing with a pinch of chopped pistachios.

NOTE

If you can't find blood oranges, any variety of orange will work; the cookies just won't have the wonderful pink icing.

DATE, CHEDDAR, AND DARK CHOCOLATE COOKIES

Trust me here. I know you are about to turn the page because you think cheddar cheese in a cookie seems wild, but it works so well. The cheese melts into the cookie to give it a slight umami flavor. The dates come in to bring sweetness and balance everything out. Then, the whole wheat flour and oats provide a hearty texture with a delicious chew. It all works together and creates a beautiful, beautiful cookie. I love offering these to others without telling them the flavor, having them guess the ingredients, and then watching the shock and amazement on their faces when they learn that the secret ingredient is cheese!

MAKES 8 LARGE COOKIES

½ cup (113 g) salted butter, softened
½ cup (108 g) brown sugar
¼ cup (50 g) granulated sugar
1 large egg, room temperature
1 teaspoon vanilla extract
¾ cup (98 g) all-purpose flour
½ cup (65 g) whole wheat flour (see Note 1)
¾ cup (68 g) rolled oats
1 tablespoon cornstarch
1 teaspoon baking soda
1 teaspoon Diamond Crystal kosher salt
½ cup (75 g) pitted Medjool dates (see Note 2)
½ cup (85 g) dark chocolate chunks, plus extra for topping
½ cup (56 g) shredded cheddar (see Notes 3 and 4)
Flaky salt, for topping

NOTES

1. If you don't have whole wheat flour, use a total of 1¼ cups (162 g) all-purpose instead!

2. If you can't find dates, feel free to substitute with raisins.

3. Use a mild or medium cheddar for a milder cookie. Use a sharp cheddar for a stronger, tangier flavor.

4. Shred your own cheese! Pre-shredded cheese contains added starches that prevent the cheese from melting.

1. Preheat the oven to 350°F (180°C). Line two baking sheets with parchment paper.
2. Place the butter, brown sugar, and granulated sugar in a large bowl. Use a stand mixer or hand mixer to mix until well combined, about 2 minutes.
3. Add the egg and vanilla extract and mix until fully combined, about 1 minute.
4. Add the all-purpose flour, whole wheat flour, oats, cornstarch, baking soda, and kosher salt. Mix until just combined, about 30 seconds.
5. Chop the dates into ¼-inch (6 mm) pieces, making sure they don't all stick together.
6. Add the dates, chocolate, and cheddar. Mix until evenly distributed throughout the dough.
7. Use a large (4-tablespoon/2-ounce) cookie scoop to scoop the dough into balls. Top each dough ball with a chocolate chunk, pressing gently into the dough.
8. Place up to four dough balls onto each baking sheet, spaced equally apart. Bake for 11 to 13 minutes, until the edges are just set.
9. Top each cookie with a pinch of flaky salt. Let the cookies cool on the baking sheets for 10 minutes and then transfer to a cooling rack to cool completely.

HOT HONEY COOKIES

Hot honey became widely popular in the late 2010s, and the world is a better place because of it. The combination of sweet and spicy is what makes it the perfect topping on pizza, fried chicken, cheese, and more—and it's also what makes it perfect for cookies. The honey sweetens the dough, and the spice provides a perfect slow-building, warm burn that lingers long after you've taken a bite. When deciding what else to add to the dough, I thought of some of my favorite pairings for hot honey in non-cookie situations: figs and goat cheese. A crunchy element was still missing, so crispy cornflakes also made the cut. The dried figs and crispy cornflakes are mixed into the dough and then the goat cheese is crumbled on top just before scooping, which swirls it into the dough while still leaving generous chunks. The combination is a delightful balance of tang, sweet, crunch, and spice.

MAKES 9 LARGE COOKIES

Crispy Cornflakes

1 tablespoon salted butter

¾ cup (40 g) cornflakes

Hot Honey Cookies

½ cup (113 g) salted butter, softened

2 tablespoons hot honey (see Note), plus extra for drizzling

⅓ cup (72 g) brown sugar

⅓ cup (66 g) granulated sugar

1 large egg, room temperature

1 teaspoon vanilla extract

1½ cups (195 g) all-purpose flour

½ teaspoon Diamond Crystal kosher salt

½ teaspoon baking powder

½ teaspoon baking soda

¼ cup (38 g) dried figs, thinly sliced

¼ cup (35 g) goat cheese

NOTE

If you want to make your own hot honey, place 2 tablespoons honey in a small microwave-safe bowl. Microwave until warm and runny, 30 to 45 seconds. Add ½ teaspoon vinegar-based hot sauce (like Frank's RedHot or Tabasco). Stir to combine and then let the honey cool completely.

1. Preheat the oven to 325°F (165°C). Line two baking sheets with parchment paper.
2. Make the cornflakes: Heat the butter in a medium pan over low heat until melted, about 2 minutes, and then add the cornflakes and stir to coat. Stir until the cornflakes are deep golden brown, about 4 minutes. Transfer to a plate to cool completely.
3. Make the cookies: Place the butter and hot honey in a large bowl. Use a stand mixer or hand mixer to mix until combined, about 1 minute.
4. Add the brown sugar and granulated sugar. Mix until combined, about 2 minutes.
5. Add the egg and vanilla extract and mix until fluffy and lighter in color, about 1 minute.
6. Add the flour, salt, baking powder, and baking soda. Mix on low just until the flour is combined.
7. Reserve nine pieces each of the crispy cornflakes and figs. Add the remaining cornflakes and figs to the dough. Mix on low until evenly distributed through the dough. Break the goat cheese into small chunks and scatter on top.
8. Use a large (4-tablespoon/2-ounce) cookie scoop to scoop the dough into balls, making sure to get a chunk of goat cheese in each scoop. Place up to five balls onto each baking sheet, spaced equally apart. Top each one with a reserved cornflake and fig, gently pressing them into the dough.
9. Bake for 10 to 12 minutes, until the edges are just set. Cool on the baking sheets for 10 minutes and then transfer to a cooling rack to cool completely.
10. For extra-spicy cookies, drizzle more hot honey on top of each cooled cookie.

DATE, PEANUT BUTTER, AND DARK CHOCOLATE COOKIES

Have you ever had a date stuffed with peanut butter, dipped in chocolate, and topped with a little flaky salt? Well, this is the cookie version of that delectable little treat. The soft, brown-sugary dough is studded with chopped dates and dark chocolate chunks and then swirled with creamy natural peanut butter. The chocolate and peanut butter melt while the cookies bake, and the dates lend a delightful chew. If you've never had a PB-stuffed date, no need—just skip right to these cookies!

MAKES 12 LARGE COOKIES

1 cup (215 g) brown sugar

¾ cup (170 g) salted butter, softened

¼ cup (50 g) granulated sugar

1 large egg plus 1 large egg yolk, room temperature

1 teaspoon vanilla extract

1¾ cups (227 g) all-purpose flour

1 teaspoon baking soda

½ teaspoon ground cinnamon

¼ teaspoon baking powder

½ cup (75 g) pitted Medjool dates

½ cup (85 g) dark chocolate chunks, plus extra for topping

½ cup (135 g) natural peanut butter, divided (see Note)

Flaky salt, for topping

NOTE

Natural peanut butter works best here! You want it to be smooth and easy to drizzle.

1. Preheat the oven to 350°F (180°C). Line two baking sheets with parchment paper.
2. Place the brown sugar, butter, and granulated sugar in a large bowl. Use a stand mixer or hand mixer to mix until well combined, about 2 minutes.
3. Add the egg, egg yolk, and vanilla extract. Mix until combined, about 1 minute.
4. Add the flour, baking soda, cinnamon, and baking powder. Mix on low until just combined with no streaks of flour remaining, about 30 seconds.
5. Chop the dates into ¼-inch (6 mm) pieces, making sure they don't all stick together.
6. Add the chocolate chunks and dates to the bowl and mix on low until evenly distributed.
7. Drizzle about ¼ cup (68 g) peanut butter over the dough. Use a large (4-tablespoon/2-ounce) cookie scoop to scoop the top layer of the dough into balls, making sure to get some of the drizzled peanut butter in each dough ball. Add the remaining peanut butter and scoop the remaining dough. Top each dough ball with a chocolate chunk, gently pressing the chunks into the dough.
8. Place up to six dough balls onto each baking sheet, spaced equally apart. Bake for 8 to 10 minutes, until the edges are just set.
9. While the cookies are still warm, sprinkle each one with a pinch of flaky salt. Let the cookies cool for 10 minutes on the baking sheets and then transfer to a cooling rack to cool completely.

SWEET CORN AND BLUEBERRY COOKIES

Corn and blueberry is a combination that is just meant to be, and after trying these cookies, I think you'll agree. Soft and chewy cornbread-esque cookies are dipped in a vibrant blueberry glaze, and the whole thing just screams summer. The corn provides a subtle savory depth, while the blueberry glaze is bright and sweet. We get the corn flavor from cornmeal, which also brings a slightly gritty texture, and from infusing the butter with corn. This step is optional, but if you love corn, it's absolutely worth it.

MAKES 9 LARGE COOKIES

Corn Cookies

1 cup (150 g) fresh or canned corn

½ cup plus 2 tablespoons (141 g) salted butter, divided

½ cup (100 g) granulated sugar

¼ cup (54 g) brown sugar

1 large egg, room temperature

1 teaspoon vanilla extract

1¼ cups (162 g) all-purpose flour

¼ cup (42 g) yellow cornmeal

½ teaspoon baking soda

½ teaspoon Diamond Crystal kosher salt

Blueberry Glaze

1 cup (150 g) fresh or frozen blueberries

1 cup (113 g) powdered sugar

1 to 2 tablespoons milk

½ teaspoon vanilla extract

NOTE

Infusing the butter is optional. To skip this step, just add ½ cup (113 g) softened butter to a large bowl and then continue with step 3.

1. Make the cookies: Preheat the oven to 350°F (180°C). Line two baking sheets with parchment paper.
2. To make the corn-infused butter (see Note), place the corn and ½ cup (113 g) butter in a medium pan over medium heat. Stir as the butter melts and comes to a simmer, about 3 minutes. Simmer, stirring occasionally, for 5 more minutes and then remove from the heat.
3. Strain the butter into a large bowl using a fine-mesh sieve. Add the remaining 2 tablespoons butter to the bowl and stir until it melts in. Transfer the corn to a small bowl.
4. Add the granulated sugar and brown sugar to the large bowl. Use a stand mixer or hand mixer to mix until combined, about 2 minutes.
5. Add the egg and vanilla extract and mix until fluffy and lighter in color, about 1 minute.
6. Add the flour, cornmeal, baking soda, and salt. Mix on low just until the flour is combined, about 30 seconds.
7. Add the corn and mix on low until just combined.
8. Use a large (4-tablespoon/2-ounce) cookie scoop to scoop the dough into balls. Place up to five dough balls onto each baking sheet, spaced equally apart.
9. Bake for 10 to 12 minutes, until the edges are just set. Let the cookies cool on the baking sheets for 10 minutes and then transfer to a cooling rack to cool completely.

recipe continues...

10. Make the glaze: Place the blueberries in a medium pan over medium heat. Stir until they begin to break down, about 3 minutes, using a rubber spatula or the back of a wooden spoon to help the blueberries break down if needed. Cook until they begin to thicken, about 3 more minutes.
11. Transfer the blueberries to a fine-mesh sieve over a small bowl and strain out the solids. Transfer the puree to the fridge to cool.
12. Place the powdered sugar in a medium shallow bowl. Add 1 tablespoon of the blueberry puree, 1 tablespoon milk, and the vanilla extract. Stir until smooth, about 1 minute. If the mixture is thick and hard to stir, add the additional tablespoon of milk. The glaze should be smooth and just thick enough to coat the back of a spoon.
13. Once the cookies are completely cooled, dip the entire top surface of each cookie in the blueberry glaze and then transfer back to the cooling rack to let any excess glaze drip off. Store any extra cookies in the fridge. It is normal for the icing to get deeper in color as they sit.

TRAIL MIX COOKIES

If you love cookies with lots of mix-ins, these are for you. These trail mix cookies are packed to the brim with fruit, nuts, and chocolate. To me, that sounds like an absolute dream, but I know those aren't everyone's ideal cookie mix-ins, or even everyone's ideal trail mix! But the beautiful thing about this cookie is that you can make it your own. Everyone likes their trail mix a little different. Some people love nuts and dried fruit (me), while others are literally just picking out the chocolate (btw, you're not being very sneaky about it). What is listed is my ideal trail mix: dark chocolate chunks, dried blueberries, raisins, pepitas, and pistachios. It's the perfect balance of crunch and sweet and bitter, imho. But if that's not your ideal, then switch it up!

MAKS 9 LARGE COOKIES

¾ cup (162 g) brown sugar

½ cup (113 g) salted butter, softened

1 large egg, room temperature

1 teaspoon vanilla extract

1 cup (130 g) whole wheat flour (see Note 1)

1 cup (90 g) rolled oats

¼ cup (42 g) dark chocolate chunks, plus extra for topping

¼ cup (40 g) dried blueberries

¼ cup (38 g) raisins

¼ cup (35 g) roasted and unsalted pepitas

¼ cup (30 g) shelled, roasted, and unsalted pistachios, chopped

1 teaspoon baking powder

1 teaspoon Diamond Crystal kosher salt

1. Preheat the oven to 325°F (165°C). Line two baking sheets with parchment paper.
2. Place the brown sugar and butter in a large bowl. Use a stand mixer or hand mixer to mix until well combined, about 3 minutes.
3. Add the egg and vanilla extract and mix until combined, about 2 minutes.
4. Add the flour, oats, chocolate chunks, blueberries, raisins, pepitas, pistachios, baking powder, and salt (see Note 2). Mix on low until just combined with no streaks of flour remaining, about 1 minute.
5. Use a large (4-tablespoon/2-ounce) cookie scoop to scoop the dough into balls. Use the palm of your hand to slightly flatten the dough balls into disks and top each with a chocolate chunk, gently pressing the chunks into the dough. Place up to five dough balls onto each baking sheet, spaced equally apart.
6. Bake for 10 to 14 minutes, until the edges are just starting to brown. Let the cookies cool on the baking sheets for 10 minutes and then transfer to a cooling rack to cool completely.

NOTES

1. If you aren't a fan of whole wheat flour or don't have it on hand, you can use all-purpose flour (1 cup/130 g) instead.

2. Add your ideal mix-ins: dried apricots, M&M's, peanuts, almonds, dried cranberries, sunflower seeds, and more. Just don't remove the oats, and be sure to keep the total volume of the mix-ins to 1¼ cups (around 185 g).

TURNING DESSERTS INTO COOKIES

I know this is a niche hobby, but there are few things I love more than tasting a dessert and figuring out a way to turn it into a cookie. This chapter shows my true, deep love for cookies. Don't get me wrong: I love each of these desserts in their typical forms, but transformed into cookies? It's game over for me. You may have tasted some of these flavors in cookie form before (like the Blueberry Muffin Cookies on page 144 or Carrot Cake Cookies on page 142), but others you'll never see coming (like the Mango Sticky Rice Cookies on page 156 or Sticky Toffee Pudding Cookies on page 170). So, flip through this chapter, pick your favorite dessert, and start there. Who knows—maybe soon, we'll share the same niche hobby!

CHILLED PEACH PIE COOKIES

I frequently get asked what my favorite cookie is. If you know me well, you know I am terrible at choosing my favorite anything. I just can't decide, OK! When it comes to cookies, I can give you a top five at best. But when summer rolls around and it's fresh peach season, that decision becomes a lot easier: It's this cookie. This soft oatmeal cookie is topped with smooth buttercream frosting and thick fresh peach slices. Then, the cookie is popped in the fridge until it's chilled, which makes it refreshing in a way that no other cookie can be. So, whether you're good at choosing favorites or not, after one bite, this will be your new favorite summer cookie, too.

MAKES 8 LARGE COOKIES

Oatmeal Cookies

½ cup (113 g) salted butter, cold
½ cup (108 g) brown sugar
½ cup (100 g) granulated sugar
1 large egg
1½ teaspoons plain Greek yogurt
1 teaspoon vanilla extract
1½ cups (195 g) all-purpose flour
¾ cup (68 g) rolled oats
1 teaspoon ground cinnamon
1 teaspoon Diamond Crystal kosher salt
¼ teaspoon baking powder

Buttercream Frosting and Peach Topping

¼ cup (56 g) salted butter, room temperature
1½ cups (170 g) powdered sugar
1 teaspoon vanilla extract
Pinch of Diamond Crystal kosher salt
1 to 2 teaspoons heavy cream or milk, room temperature
2 medium fresh peaches, sliced (see Note)

1. Preheat the oven to 325°F (165°C). Line two baking sheets with parchment paper.
2. Make the cookies: Place the butter, brown sugar, and granulated sugar in a large bowl. Use a stand mixer or hand mixer to mix until the butter is broken down and fully combined with the sugar, about 3 minutes.
3. Add the egg, yogurt, and vanilla extract. Mix until fully combined, about 1 minute.
4. Add the flour, oats, cinnamon, salt, and baking powder. Mix on low just until no streaks of flour remain, about 1 minute.
5. Use a large (4-tablespoon/2-ounce) cookie scoop to scoop the dough into balls. Place up to four dough balls onto each baking sheet, spaced equally apart. Use the palm of your hand to slightly flatten each dough ball into a disk.
6. Bake for 9 to 12 minutes, until the edges are just starting to set. The middles should still look slightly doughy. Let the cookies cool on the baking sheets for 5 minutes and then transfer to a plate in the fridge to cool completely, about 1 hour.
7. Meanwhile, make the frosting: Place the butter in a large bowl. Use a stand mixer or hand mixer to mix until smooth and creamy, about 2 minutes.
8. Add the powdered sugar, vanilla extract, and salt. Mix until fully combined and smooth, about 2 minutes. Add 1 teaspoon of the heavy cream and mix until smooth, about 1 minute. If the frosting is still very thick and not easily spreadable, add the additional teaspoon of cream and mix again.

9. Remove the cookies from the fridge and use an offset spatula to spread 1 to 2 tablespoons of frosting on each cookie in an even layer. Store the cookies in the fridge until ready to serve. Just before serving, top each with a slice or two of fresh peach. Store any extra cookies in the fridge.

NOTE

If it isn't peach season or you can't find a fresh peach anywhere, canned peaches will do, though they're definitely not as good.

CINNAMON ROLL SNICKERDOODLE COOKIES

I absolutely love a fresh cinnamon roll, so it only felt right to turn it into a cookie. The result is a soft snickerdoodle base studded with pockets of brown sugar–cinnamon "filling," all topped with a smooth cream cheese frosting. If you aren't already convinced that these will be life-altering cookies, I don't know what else to tell you. Take my word for it and thank me later. <3

MAKES 8 LARGE COOKIES

Brown Sugar–Cinnamon "Filling"

¼ cup (54 g) brown sugar

2 tablespoons salted butter, softened

¾ teaspoon ground cinnamon

Snickerdoodle Cookies

½ cup (113 g) salted butter, softened

½ cup (108 g) brown sugar

¼ cup (50 g) plus 1 tablespoon granulated sugar, divided

1 large egg, room temperature

1 teaspoon vanilla extract

1¾ cups (228 g) all-purpose flour

½ tablespoon cornstarch

½ teaspoon baking soda

½ teaspoon Diamond Crystal kosher salt

1 teaspoon ground cinnamon

Cream Cheese Frosting

1½ cups (170 g) powdered sugar

2 ounces (56 g) cream cheese, softened

1 to 2 teaspoons milk

½ teaspoon vanilla extract

1. Preheat the oven to 350°F (180°C). Line a large plate and two baking sheets with parchment paper.
2. Make the "filling": Place the brown sugar, butter, and cinnamon in a small bowl and use a spoon to mix until combined, about 2 minutes. Use your fingers to drop small chunks of the mixture onto the plate. Transfer to the freezer to harden for 15 minutes while you make the dough (see Note).
3. Meanwhile, make the cookies: Place the butter, the brown sugar, and ¼ cup (50 g) granulated sugar in a large bowl. Use a stand mixer or hand mixer to mix until well combined, about 2 minutes.
4. Add the egg and vanilla extract, and mix until combined, about 1 minute.
5. Add the flour, cornstarch, baking soda, and salt. Mix until just combined, about 30 seconds.
6. Remove the brown sugar–cinnamon chunks from the freezer. Add them to the dough and mix slowly until just combined.
7. Mix the remaining 1 tablespoon granulated sugar and the cinnamon in a small bowl.
8. Use a large (4-tablespoon/2-ounce) cookie scoop to scoop the dough into balls. Roll each dough ball between the palms of your hands until smooth and then drop it into the cinnamon sugar and roll to coat.

recipe continues...

9. Place up to four dough balls onto each baking sheet, spaced equally apart. Bake for 8 to 10 minutes, until the cookies are just set, possibly still slightly doughy. Let the cookies cool on the baking sheets for 10 minutes and then transfer to a cooling rack to cool completely.
10. Meanwhile, make the frosting: Place the powdered sugar, cream cheese, 1 teaspoon milk, and vanilla extract in a medium bowl. Use a whisk to mix until smooth, about 2 minutes. If the frosting is too thick, add another teaspoon of milk and mix again.
11. When the cookies are completely cool, use a piping bag to pipe about 1 tablespoon of frosting onto each cookie. Store any extra cookies in the fridge.

NOTE

Putting the "filling" in the freezer is essential. This ensures it doesn't fully melt into the cookies in the oven and creates the beautiful big pockets of brown sugar–cinnamon goodness that make these cookies spectacular.

KEY LIME PIE COOKIES

There are a handful of cookies that, after just one bite, you realize you'll never forget, and this is one of them. All the best flavors of key lime pie are packed into this recipe: Soft graham cracker cookies are topped with a creamy key lime custard-like mixture that is zesty and not too sweet. These cookies are practically mini key lime pies, and you'll never need the real deal again.

MAKES 7 LARGE COOKIES

Graham Cracker Cookies

½ cup (113 g) salted butter, softened

½ cup (180 g) brown sugar

¼ cup (50 g) granulated sugar

1 large egg, room temperature

1 teaspoon vanilla extract

1¼ cups (162 g) all-purpose flour

½ cup (50 g) graham cracker crumbs (about 3½ sheets)

½ teaspoon baking soda

½ teaspoon Diamond Crystal kosher salt

Key Lime Filling

1 cup (240 ml) heavy cream

1 tablespoon honey

Zest of 1 lime (about 2 teaspoons)

3 tablespoons lime juice (from about 1½ limes)

½ teaspoon vanilla extract

Pinch of Diamond Crystal kosher salt

Lime zest or slices for topping, optional

1. Preheat the oven to 350°F (180°C). Line two baking sheets with parchment paper.
2. Make the cookies: Place the butter, brown sugar, and granulated sugar in a large bowl. Use a stand mixer or hand mixer to mix until well combined.
3. Add the egg and vanilla extract. Mix until well combined and fluffy, about 1 minute.
4. Add the flour, graham cracker crumbs, baking soda, and salt. Mix on low just until no streaks of flour remain, about 30 seconds.
5. Use a large (4-tablespoon/2-ounce) cookie scoop to scoop the dough into balls. Place up to four dough balls onto each baking sheet, spaced equally apart.
6. Bake for 8 to 10 minutes, until the edges are just starting to set. Remove from the oven and immediately use a measuring spoon or cup that is just smaller than the cookies to make an indent in each cookie, leaving about a ½-inch (1 cm) border. Let cool.
7. Meanwhile, make the filling: Bring the heavy cream, honey, and lime zest to a boil in a medium pot over medium heat. Boil, stirring occasionally, for 5 minutes. The mixture will thicken slightly but still be quite runny.
8. Turn off the heat and add the lime juice, vanilla extract, and salt. Stir until combined, about 30 seconds. The mixture should be thicker, but still pourable. Carefully pour the hot mixture into the indent of each cookie, filling it to the top. Cover the baking sheets with plastic wrap and transfer to the fridge to chill for at least 1 hour to let the filling set up.
9. Serve the cookies directly from the fridge. Top with lime zest or thin slices of lime, if desired. Store any extra cookies in the fridge.

BANANA PUDDING COOKIES

My friends and family members who tried this cookie when I was testing the recipe said it was the best cookie they've had in a long time. That may be an indictment of my other work, but more likely (I hope) it's a testament to just how good this cookie is. It really does taste like banana pudding in cookie form. I know that's trite, but it's true. It's a vanilla cookie with vanilla wafer crumbs in the dough and rolled on the outside, topped with a light and creamy pudding frosting and slices of fresh banana. I am not a fan of artificial banana flavor, so the only banana flavor here comes from the fresh bananas (which is true for most banana puddings, too).

MAKES 8 LARGE COOKIES

Vanilla Wafer Cookies

½ cup (113 g) salted butter, softened

½ cup (100 g) granulated sugar

¼ cup (54 g) brown sugar

1 large egg, room temperature

1 teaspoon vanilla extract

1¼ cups (162 g) all-purpose flour

¾ cup (75 g) vanilla wafer crumbs, divided (see Note)

1½ teaspoons cornstarch

1 teaspoon Diamond Crystal kosher salt

½ teaspoon baking soda

Pudding Frosting

One 3.4-ounce (96 g) box instant vanilla pudding mix

1 cup (240 ml) milk

1 teaspoon vanilla extract

1 cup (240 ml) heavy cream

2 large bananas, peeled and thinly sliced

NOTE

Use vanilla wafers, such as Nilla Wafers, not cream-filled ones.

1. Preheat the oven to 350°F (180°C). Line two baking sheets with parchment paper.
2. Make the cookies: Place the butter, granulated sugar, and brown sugar in a large bowl. Use a stand mixer or hand mixer to mix until well combined, about 2 minutes.
3. Add the egg and vanilla extract. Mix until combined and fluffy, about 1 minute.
4. Add the flour, ½ cup (50 g) vanilla wafer crumbs, cornstarch, salt, and baking soda. Mix on low until just combined, about 30 seconds.
5. Place the remaining vanilla wafer crumbs in a shallow bowl.
6. Use a large (4-tablespoon/2-ounce) cookie scoop to scoop the dough into balls. Roll each dough ball in the palms of your hands until smooth and then roll it in the vanilla wafer crumbs to coat.
7. Place up to four dough balls onto each baking sheet, spaced equally apart. Bake for 9 to 11 minutes, until the edges are just set. Let the cookies cool on the baking sheets for 10 minutes and then transfer to a cooling rack to cool completely.
8. Make the frosting: Place the pudding mix, milk, and vanilla extract in a medium bowl. Use a whisk to mix until no clumps remain, about 1 minute.

9. Place the heavy cream in a separate medium bowl. Use a hand mixer or whisk to beat until stiff peaks form, about 5 minutes. Scoop half of the whipped cream into the pudding mixture and gently mix until combined, about 1 minute. Add the remaining whipped cream and mix gently until combined, about 30 seconds.
10. Use a spoon or cookie scoop to scoop 2 to 3 tablespoons of frosting onto each cooled cookie. Top each cookie with a few banana slices.
11. Store any extra cookies in an airtight containter in the fridge. Alternatively, store the cookies (without the topping) in an airtight container in the fridge and the pudding frosting in another airtight container in the fridge. Assemble just before serving.

CARROT CAKE COOKIES

This recipe holds a very special place in my heart. It's the first cookie recipe I ever shared on my website, aka the first cookie recipe I ever developed! And it is, shockingly, still one of my favorites. It's honestly kind of a miracle that these turned out as well as they did, because I developed the recipe back when I understood very little about cookie science and was truly winging it. I remember having to test these quite a few times before I got them right, but I got them very right and have never looked back. You should also know that I am a sucker for carrot cake. I truly think it is one of the best desserts on the planet, and putting it in cookie form makes it even better. The cream cheese frosting (a nonnegotiable for carrot cake) can either be stuffed in the center of the cookie or piped on top! You really can't go wrong with these. So, without further ado, here are my first cookies ever.

MAKES 9 LARGE COOKIES

Cream Cheese Filling (see Note)

2 ounces (57 g) cream cheese, room temperature

2 tablespoons salted butter, room temperature

½ teaspoon vanilla extract

1 cup (113 g) powdered sugar

Pinch of Diamond Crystal kosher salt

Carrot Cake Cookies

2 large carrots, washed and peeled

¾ cup plus 2 tablespoons (188 g) brown sugar

½ cup (113 g) salted butter, cold and cubed

1 large egg

1 teaspoon vanilla extract

1¾ cups (227 g) all-purpose flour

1 tablespoon cornstarch

1 teaspoon Diamond Crystal kosher salt

½ teaspoon baking soda

½ teaspoon ground cinnamon

¼ cup (30 g) unsalted pecans, crushed, optional

1. Make the filling: Place the cream cheese, butter, and vanilla extract in a large bowl. Use a stand mixer or hand mixer to mix until well combined, about 2 minutes. Add the powdered sugar and salt and mix until combined and smooth, about 2 minutes.
2. Use a small (1-tablespoon/½-ounce) cookie scoop to scoop the frosting onto a small baking sheet or large plate lined with parchment paper. Transfer to the freezer to harden for at least 15 minutes.
3. Make the cookies: Finely grate the carrots and then transfer to a paper towel or tea towel. Let the towel absorb some of the juice from the carrots while you make the dough.
4. Place the brown sugar and butter in a large bowl. Use a stand mixer or hand mixer to mix until well combined, starting on low and then increasing the speed when the butter starts to break down, about 3 minutes.
5. Add the egg and vanilla extract and mix until fully combined, about 2 minutes.
6. Add the flour, cornstarch, salt, baking soda, and cinnamon. Mix on low until just combined, about 30 seconds.
7. Use your hands to squeeze any extra juice from the carrots. Add ¾ cup (90 g) of the carrots to the dough along with the pecans, if using, and then mix on low until the carrots are just distributed throughout the dough.
8. Cover the dough with plastic wrap and transfer to the fridge to chill for 30 minutes. Preheat the oven to 350°F (180°C). Line two baking sheets with parchment paper.

9. Remove the dough from the fridge and the frosting from the freezer. Use a large (4-tablespoon/2-ounce) cookie scoop to scoop the dough into balls. For each ball, with the dough still in the cookie scoop, use your fingers to make an indent in the dough. Add a chunk of frozen frosting to the center and then close the dough around the frosting, making sure it's completely sealed.
10. Place up to five dough balls onto each baking sheet, spaced equally apart. Bake for 10 to 12 minutes, until the outsides are slightly golden brown and just set. Let the cookies cool on the baking sheets for 20 minutes and then transfer to a cooling rack to cool completely. Store any extra cookies in the fridge.

NOTE

If you would like to frost the cookies rather than stuffing them, double the frosting recipe. Transfer the frosting to a piping bag and then, once the cookies are completely cool, pipe 1 to 2 tablespoons of frosting onto each cookie.

BLUEBERRY MUFFIN COOKIES

My brother was obsessed with blueberry muffins growing up (and he still is), so I have countless memories of baking them, usually from a boxed mix, and eating them all in one go. The blueberry muffin is the perfect muffin to turn into a cookie. I wanted these cookies to be extra soft, so I add cream cheese to the dough. Cream cheese isn't a typical ingredient in cookie dough, but it provides a softness that is hard to replicate. Fresh blueberries are gently folded into the dough, and each cookie is topped with a generous pile of buttery streusel, as all good blueberry muffins are. They are finished with a smooth (optional) icing. Forget muffins: These cookies are all you need for breakfast.

MAKES 10 LARGE COOKIES

Blueberry Muffin Cookies

¾ cup (150 g) granulated sugar
½ cup (113 g) salted butter, softened
¼ cup (56 g) cream cheese, softened
¼ cup (54 g) brown sugar
1 large egg, room temperature
1 teaspoon vanilla extract
1⅔ cups (215 g) all-purpose flour
1 teaspoon baking powder
1 teaspoon Diamond Crystal kosher salt
½ teaspoon baking soda
1 cup (150 g) fresh blueberries (see Notes)

Streusel Topping

½ cup (65 g) all-purpose flour
¼ cup (56 g) salted butter, softened
¼ cup (50 g) granulated sugar
Pinch of Diamond Crystal kosher salt

Icing (optional)

1 cup (113 g) powdered sugar
1 teaspoon milk
¼ teaspoon vanilla extract

1. Preheat the oven to 350°F (180°C). Line two baking sheets with parchment paper.
2. Make the cookies: Place the granulated sugar, butter, cream cheese, and brown sugar in a large bowl. Use a hand mixer or stand mixer to mix until well combined, about 3 minutes.
3. Add the egg and vanilla extract and mix until fluffy and lighter in color, about 2 minutes.
4. Add the flour, baking powder, salt, and baking soda. Mix on low until just combined.
5. Add the blueberries and gently mix with a rubber spatula, trying not to burst any of the blueberries. Mix just until they are evenly distributed throughout the dough.
6. Use a large (4-tablespoon/2-ounce) cookie scoop to scoop the dough into balls. Place five balls onto each baking sheet, spaced equally apart. Use the palm of your hand to slightly flatten each ball.
7. Make the topping: Use a fork to combine the flour, butter, sugar, and salt in a medium bowl. The streusel should stick together when squeezed into a ball but crumble when you run your fingers through it. Place 1 tablespoon of the streusel on top of each ball, pressing it in slightly so it sticks.
8. Bake for 10 to 13 minutes, until the edges are just starting to set. Let the cookies cool on the baking sheets for 10 minutes and then transfer to a cooling rack to cool completely.

9. Make the icing, if desired: Whisk the powdered sugar, milk, and vanilla extract in a small bowl until smooth. If the icing is too thick, add another splash of milk. If it's too runny, add more powdered sugar. Drizzle the icing over each cookie.

NOTES

1. Frozen blueberries don't work well here. They contain a lot more water and will change the consistency of the cookie.

2. Since these cookies use fresh blueberries, they are best enjoyed within 2 days.

LEMON MERINGUE COOKIES

I used to think I wasn't a meringue person, but I've found I'm just not a fan of baked, hard meringue. But the torched, fluffy stuff? It's delightful. For this recipe, we're making a soft lemon sugar cookie topped with a layer of lemon curd and a small mountain of fresh meringue. The meringue is torched until golden brown to create the perfect finishing touch, and the result is one of the most stunning cookies I've ever made—and one of the most delicious, too.

MAKES 7 LARGE COOKIES

Lemon Cookies

½ cup (100 g) granulated sugar

Zest of 1 lemon (about 1 tablespoon)

½ cup (113 g) salted butter, softened

¼ cup (54 g) brown sugar

2 large egg yolks, room temperature

2 tablespoons sour cream

2 teaspoons vanilla extract

1½ cups (195 g) all-purpose flour

1 tablespoon cornstarch

1 teaspoon Diamond Crystal kosher salt

½ teaspoon baking powder

¼ cup (56 g) lemon curd

Meringue Topping

2 large egg whites

¼ cup (50 g) granulated sugar

½ teaspoon vanilla extract

NOTE

Meringue is best enjoyed on the day it's made.

1. Preheat the oven to 350°F (180°C). Line two baking sheets with parchment paper.
2. Make the cookies: Place the sugar and lemon zest in a large bowl. Use your fingers to rub the lemon zest into the sugar, releasing the lemon oil.
3. Add the butter and brown sugar. Use a stand mixer or hand mixer to mix until well combined, about 2 minutes.
4. Add the egg yolks, sour cream, and vanilla extract. Mix until combined and fluffy, about 1 minute.
5. Add the flour, cornstarch, salt, and baking powder. Mix on low just until no streaks of flour remain, about 30 seconds.
6. Use a large (4-tablespoon/2-ounce) cookie scoop to scoop the dough into balls. Place up to four dough balls onto each baking sheet, spaced equally apart.
7. Bake for 9 to 12 minutes, until the edges are just set. Immediately after removing the cookies from the oven, use the back of a spoon to gently indent each cookie about ¼-inch (6 mm) deep. Let the cookies cool on the baking sheets for 10 minutes and then transfer to a cooling rack to cool completely.
8. Meanwhile, make the meringue: Add 1 inch (2.5 cm) of water to a large pot and bring to a boil. Add the egg whites and sugar to a heat-safe bowl that fits snugly into the pot and whisk to combine, about 1 minute. Place the bowl into the pot, making sure the bottom of the bowl doesn't touch the boiling water.

9. Whisk until the sugar dissolves, 3 to 5 minutes. Carefully pour the mixture into a large bowl and add the vanilla extract. Use a stand mixer or hand mixer to mix until stiff peaks form, about 5 minutes.

10. Once the cookies are completely cooled, add about 1½ teaspoons lemon curd into the indent of each cookie. Then, top with about ¼ cup (30 g) meringue. Use a kitchen torch to carefully torch the meringue until golden brown, about 5 seconds.

RASPBERRY CHEESECAKE COOKIES

The best cheesecakes have a thick graham cracker crust (imo), and that's exactly what these cookies deliver. We're starting with a thick graham cracker cookie that is extremely reminiscent of a cheesecake crust, topping it with a generous layer of creamy and smooth cream cheese frosting, and then finishing it with a tart raspberry drizzle that perfectly balances out the sweetness of the cookie. If you too are a sucker for cheesecakes with lots of graham cracker goodness, these cookies are for you.

MAKES 7 LARGE COOKIES

Graham Cracker Cookies

½ cup (113 g) salted butter, cold
½ cup (108 g) brown sugar
¼ cup (50 g) granulated sugar
1 large egg
½ teaspoon vanilla extract
1¼ cups (162 g) all-purpose flour
½ cup (50 g) graham cracker crumbs (about 3½ sheets)
½ teaspoon baking soda
½ teaspoon Diamond Crystal kosher salt

Cream Cheese Frosting

4 ounces (113 g) cream cheese, room temperature
¼ cup (56 g) salted butter, room temperature
1½ cups (170 g) powdered sugar
½ teaspoon vanilla extract

Raspberry Topping

1 cup (120 g) fresh or frozen raspberries
1 tablespoon water
1 teaspoon cornstarch

1. Preheat the oven to 350°F (180°C). Line two baking sheets with parchment paper.
2. Make the cookies: Cut the butter into ½-inch (1 cm) cubes and place them in a large bowl. Add the brown sugar and granulated sugar and use a stand mixer or hand mixer to mix until the butter is broken down and fully combined with the sugar, about 3 minutes.
3. Add the egg and vanilla extract and mix until fully combined and lighter in color, about 1 minute.
4. Add the flour, graham cracker crumbs, baking soda, and salt. Mix on low until just combined, about 1 minute.
5. Use a large (4-tablespoon/2-ounce) cookie scoop to scoop the dough into balls. Place up to four dough balls onto each baking sheet, spaced equally apart. Use the palm of your hand to slightly flatten each dough ball into a disk.
6. Bake for 9 to 11 minutes, until the edges are just set. Let the cookies cool on the baking sheets for 5 minutes and then transfer to a cooling rack to cool completely.
7. Meanwhile, make the frosting: Place the cream cheese and butter in a large bowl. Use a stand mixer or hand mixer to mix until well combined, about 2 minutes. Add the powdered sugar and vanilla extract and mix until smooth, about 2 more minutes. Transfer the frosting to a piping bag with a round, open tip.

8. Make the topping: Heat a medium pan over medium heat. Add the raspberries and stir until they begin to break down, about 5 minutes. Whisk the water and cornstarch in a small bowl. Once the raspberry mixture begins to bubble, stir in the cornstarch slurry. Continue to stir until the mixture thickens enough to coat the back of a spoon, about 3 minutes.
9. Transfer the raspberry mixture to a small bowl and place it in the fridge until cool, about 20 minutes.
10. When the cookies are completely cool, use a piping bag to pipe 1 to 2 tablespoons of frosting onto each cookie. Then, drizzle on the cooled raspberry topping. Store any extra cookies in the fridge.

CORNBREAD COOKIES

Cornbread is one of the best additions to a meal. And just because this recipe turns it into a cookie doesn't mean it can't still accompany your bowl of chili (OK, maybe that's too far). This cookie captures all the flavors of cornbread: Cornmeal is added to the dough to provide the distinctive corn flavor and gritty cornbread texture, and then it's topped with a smooth honey buttercream frosting that really drives the comparison home.

MAKES 7 LARGE COOKIES

Cornbread Cookies

½ cup (113 g) salted butter, softened

½ cup (108 g) brown sugar

¼ cup (50 g) granulated sugar

1 large egg, room temperature

½ teaspoon vanilla extract

1¼ cups (162 g) all-purpose flour

½ cup (75 g) yellow cornmeal

1 teaspoon cornstarch

½ teaspoon baking powder

½ teaspoon Diamond Crystal kosher salt

Honey Buttercream

¼ cup (56 g) salted butter, softened

1 tablespoon honey (see Note)

1 cup (113 g) powdered sugar

1 teaspoon vanilla extract

Pinch of Diamond Crystal kosher salt

1. Preheat the oven to 350°F (180°C). Line two baking sheets with parchment paper.
2. Make the cookies: Place the butter, brown sugar, and granulated sugar in a large bowl. Use a stand or hand mixer to combine, about 2 minutes.
3. Add the egg and vanilla extract and mix until fully combined, about 1 minute.
4. Add the flour, cornmeal, cornstarch, baking powder, and salt. Mix on low until just combined, about 30 seconds.
5. Use a large (4-tablespoon/2-ounce) cookie scoop to scoop the dough into balls. Place up to four dough balls onto each baking sheet, spaced equally apart. Bake for 9 to 11 minutes, until the edges are just starting to brown.
6. Let the cookies cool on the baking sheets for 5 minutes and then transfer to a cooling rack.
7. Meanwhile, make the buttercream: Place the butter and honey in a medium bowl. Use a hand mixer or whisk to mix until well combined, about 1 minute. Add the powdered sugar, vanilla extract, and salt. Mix to form a smooth frosting, about 1 minute.
8. Top each cooled cookie with 1 tablespoon of frosting.

NOTE

For extra honey flavor, top each frosted cookie with a drizzle of honey.

APPLE CRISP COOKIES

Apple crisp is an underrated dessert. Fresh apples, tossed in spices, topped with a mountain of streusel—I mean, what's not to like? And if you're into the crisp, I promise you'll love the cookie version as well. A soft brown sugar dough is stuffed with fresh apples tossed in cinnamon and then each dough ball is topped with its own mountain of streusel. A smooth maple icing is drizzled on top to bring everything together.

MAKES 9 LARGE COOKIES

Apple Snickerdoodles

1 medium red or green apple, peeled and chopped into ¼-inch (6 mm) cubes

½ teaspoon ground cinnamon

½ cup (113 g) salted butter, softened

½ cup (100 g) granulated sugar

¼ cup (54 g) brown sugar

1 large egg, room temperature

1 teaspoon vanilla extract

1¾ cups (228 g) all-purpose flour

½ teaspoon baking soda

½ teaspoon Diamond Crystal kosher salt

Streusel

¼ cup (56 g) salted butter, softened

¼ cup (54 g) brown sugar

¼ cup (23 g) rolled oats

2 tablespoons all-purpose flour

½ teaspoon ground cinnamon

Pinch of Diamond Crystal kosher salt

Maple Icing

½ cup (56 g) powdered sugar

1 tablespoon maple syrup

Splash of milk, if needed

1. Preheat the oven to 350°F (180°C). Line two baking sheets with parchment paper.
2. Make the cookies: Place the apple and cinnamon in a small bowl and toss to combine.
3. Place the butter, granulated sugar, and brown sugar in a large bowl. Use a hand mixer or stand mixer to mix until well combined, about 2 minutes.
4. Add the egg and vanilla extract and mix until well combined, about 1 minute.
5. Add the flour, baking soda, and salt. Mix on low until just combined, about 30 seconds.
6. Use a large (4-tablespoon/2-ounce) cookie scoop to scoop the dough into balls. For each ball, with the dough still in the cookie scoop, use your fingers to make an indent in the dough. Add about 1 teaspoon of apple cubes to the center and then close the dough around the apples, making sure it's completely sealed.
7. Place up to five dough balls onto each baking sheet, spaced equally apart.
8. Make the streusel: Place the butter, brown sugar, oats, flour, cinnamon, and salt in a small bowl. Use a rubber spatula or your hands to mix until well combined, about 1 minute. The mixture should stick together when squeezed into a ball but crumble when you run your fingers through it.
9. Place a heaping tablespoon of streusel on top of each dough ball, pressing it in so it sticks.
10. Bake for 9 to 11 minutes, until the edges are just starting to set. Let the cookies cool on the baking sheets for 10 minutes and then transfer to a cooling rack to cool completely.

11. Make the maple icing: Place the powdered sugar and maple syrup in a small bowl. Use a whisk or fork to mix until combined, about 1 minute. If the icing is very thick, add a splash of milk and stir.

12. Once the cookies have cooled completely, drizzle about 1 teaspoon of icing on top of each cookie. Store any extra cookies in the fridge for up to 2 days.

CRÈME BRÛLÉE COOKIES

These cookies are a dream. A brown sugar dough is topped with a smooth vanilla custard. Then, just like crème brûlée, sugar is sprinkled on top and torched until it melts. Once it cools, the melted sugar creates a hard shell across the top of the cookie. You can eat it like a normal cookie with your hands, but I recommend eating it on a plate with a spoon so you can have the satisfying crack of the hard shell and scoop up every bit of custard on the plate.

MAKES 10 LARGE COOKIES

Crème Brûlée Custard

1 cup (240 ml) whole milk

2 large egg yolks, room temperature

1 tablespoon plus 10 teaspoons granulated sugar, divided

½ tablespoon cornstarch

1 teaspoon vanilla extract

Brown Sugar Cookies

½ cup plus 2 tablespoons (141 g) salted butter, softened

¾ cup (162 g) brown sugar

¼ cup (50 g) granulated sugar

1 large egg, room temperature

1 teaspoon vanilla extract

1¾ cups (227 g) all-purpose flour

½ teaspoon Diamond Crystal kosher salt

½ teaspoon baking powder

½ teaspoon baking soda

1. Make the custard: Place the milk, egg yolks, 1 tablespoon granulated sugar, and cornstarch in a medium pot. Whisk until well combined. Place the pot over medium-low heat. Whisk frequently until the mixture thickens enough to coat the back of a spoon, 6 to 8 minutes.
2. Remove from the heat, add the vanilla extract, and whisk until smooth. Transfer to a medium bowl and cover with plastic wrap so that the wrap touches the surface of the custard. Transfer to the fridge to cool completely, about 30 minutes.
3. Preheat the oven to 375°F (190°C). Line two baking sheets with parchment paper.
4. Make the cookies: Place the butter, brown sugar, and granulated sugar in a large bowl. Use a stand mixer or hand mixer to mix until fully combined, about 2 minutes.
5. Add the egg and vanilla extract and mix until fluffy and lighter in color, about 1 minute.
6. Add the flour, salt, baking powder, and baking soda. Mix on low just until the flour is combined, about 30 seconds.
7. Use a large (4-tablespoon/2-ounce) cookie scoop to scoop the dough into balls. Place up to five dough balls onto each baking sheet, spaced equally apart.
8. Bake for 10 to 12 minutes, until the edges are just set. Let the cookies cool on the baking sheets for 10 minutes and then transfer to a cooling rack to cool completely.

9. Top each cooled cookie with 1 to 2 tablespoons of custard and then 1 teaspoon of granulated sugar on top of the custard. Use a kitchen torch to melt the sugar until it turns golden brown. If you don't have a torch, place the cookies in the oven with the highest broil setting on. Watch carefully and cook just until the sugar melts. Let cool completely. Store any extra cookies in the fridge.

MANGO STICKY RICE COOKIES

I grew up eating mango sticky rice often—my parents had a bamboo basket to steam the rice, and it was always such a delight. So, when I was brainstorming ideas for this chapter, mango sticky rice was an obvious yes. But how do you make a rice-based dessert into a cookie? By adding sticky rice straight into the cookie dough. I thought it was crazy at first, but it does exactly what you would hope: It creates a soft, satisfying, chewy texture that has me questioning why we haven't been putting rice into all of our cookies. The dough also contains coconut milk and shredded coconut to really build the coconut rice flavor. Then, to tie it all together, the cookies are topped with a generous dollop of whipped cream, fresh mango slices, and a pinch of toasted sesame seeds. It's kind of a fork-and-knife situation, or at least a several-napkin situation, but you'll be hooked after one bite.

MAKES 10 LARGE COOKIES

Coconut Rice Cookies

¾ cup (162 g) brown sugar

½ cup (113 g) salted butter, softened

¼ cup (60 ml) canned full-fat coconut milk

1 large egg, room temperature

1 teaspoon vanilla extract

1½ cups (195 g) all-purpose flour

1 teaspoon Diamond Crystal kosher salt

½ teaspoon baking soda

1 cup (60 g) unsweetened shredded coconut

½ cup (120 g) cooked short grain rice, room temperature

Topping

1 cup (240 ml) heavy cream

1 teaspoon granulated sugar

1 medium mango (see Note)

1 teaspoon toasted sesame seeds

NOTE

If you can, use a champagne (or Ataulfo) mango. They are sweeter and less fibrous than other mangos, which makes them perfect for these cookies.

1. Preheat the oven to 350°F (180°C). Line two baking sheets with parchment paper.
2. Make the cookies: Place the brown sugar and butter in a large bowl. Use a stand mixer or hand mixer to mix until fully combined, about 2 minutes.
3. Add the coconut milk, egg, and vanilla extract and mix until fully combined, about 1 minute.
4. Add the flour, salt, and baking soda. Mix on low just until the flour is combined, about 30 seconds.
5. Add the coconut and rice and mix on low until just combined.
6. Use a large (4-tablespoon/2-ounce) cookie scoop to scoop the dough into balls. Place up to five dough balls onto each baking sheet, spaced equally apart.
7. Bake for 10 to 12 minutes, until the edges are just set. Let the cookies cool on the baking sheets for 10 minutes and then transfer to a cooling rack or the fridge to cool completely.
8. Make the topping: Place the heavy cream and sugar in a medium bowl. Use a stand mixer or hand mixer to mix until soft peaks form, about 4 minutes.
9. Peel and cut the mango into thin strips.
10. To assemble the cookies, top each one with a dollop of whipped cream. Add a few mango slices and a sprinkle of sesame seeds. Store any extra cookies in the fridge for up to 2 days. After 2 days, the rice starts to harden.

ALMOND CROISSANT COOKIES

An almond croissant cookie that actually tastes like an almond croissant? Sign me up. OK, so the texture of this cookie is obviously different from a croissant, but the taste is spot on. The dough is stuffed with frangipane, a creamy almond filling used in many French desserts, including almond croissants. The frangipane is made with almond flour and almond extract, giving these cookies the perfect almond flavor. The dough is topped with a bit of frangipane and lots of sliced almonds before baking and then dusted with powdered sugar afterward, giving these cookies the iconic almond croissant look. Go ahead and turn your kitchen into a French bakery for the day and everyone will thank you.

MAKES 16 LARGE COOKIES

Frangipane

1¾ cups (168 g) almond flour

⅔ cup (133 g) granulated sugar

1 large egg, room temperature

2 tablespoons salted butter, melted

½ teaspoon almond extract

Almond Cookies

1 cup (227 g) salted butter, softened

1 cup (200 g) granulated sugar

⅔ cup (76 g) powdered sugar, plus more for dusting

2 large eggs, room temperature

1 teaspoon almond extract

1 teaspoon vanilla extract

3 cups (390 g) all-purpose flour

1½ teaspoons Diamond Crystal kosher salt

1 teaspoon baking powder

1 teaspoon baking soda

½ cup (43 g) sliced almonds

1. Preheat the oven to 350°F (180°C). Line two baking sheets with parchment paper.
2. Make the frangipane: Place the almond flour and sugar in a medium bowl and mix to combine, about 1 minute. Add the egg, butter, and almond extract. Use a rubber spatula to mix until a smooth, thick paste forms, about 1 minute. Cover the bowl and transfer to the fridge to cool, about 15 minutes.
3. Make the cookies: Place the butter, granulated sugar, and powdered sugar in a large bowl. Use a stand mixer or hand mixer to mix until well combined, about 3 minutes.
4. Add the eggs, almond extract, and vanilla extract. Mix until well combined and fluffy, about 1 minute.
5. Add the flour, salt, baking powder, and baking soda. Mix on low just until no streaks of flour remain, about 30 seconds.
6. Take the frangipane out of the fridge. It should be slightly firmer but still malleable.
7. Place the sliced almonds in a shallow bowl.
8. Use a small (1-tablespoon/½-ounce) cookie scoop or measuring spoon to scoop the frangipane into balls. Use a large (4-tablespoon/2-ounce) cookie scoop to scoop the dough into balls. Use your fingers to make a hole in each dough ball and place one ball of frangipane inside before closing the dough around the frangipane.

9. Top each dough ball with about ½ teaspoon of frangipane and then dip it in the almonds so the top half of the dough ball is covered.
10. Place up to four dough balls onto each baking sheet, spaced equally apart. Bake for 10 to 13 minutes, until the cookies are just barely set. Let the cookies cool on the baking sheets for 5 minutes and then transfer to a cooling rack to cool completely.
11. Repeat step 10 to bake the remaining dough.
12. Top each cooled cookie with a dusting of powdered sugar.

BANANA CREAM PIE COOKIES

My biggest complaint about most banana cookies is that they have a very cakey texture, like something halfway between banana bread and a cookie. While there certainly is a time and place for cakey cookies, I wanted a banana cookie that was soft and chewy, and this cookie really delivers. The secret ingredient is the instant pudding mix. Its subtle vanilla pudding flavor nods to the cream pie element of the cookie, but the biggest thing it provides is moisture. I tested these with banana-flavored instant pudding mix, but I hate artificial banana flavor, so it just didn't work. Vanilla pudding mix works best here, and combined with fresh banana, vanilla wafers, white chocolate chips, and mini marshmallows, it makes these cookies pretty unforgettable.

MAKES 20 LARGE COOKIES

1½ cups (323 g) brown sugar

1 cup (227 g) salted butter, softened

½ cup (113 g) mashed banana (from about 1 large banana)

One 3.4-ounce (96 g) box vanilla instant pudding mix

2 large eggs, room temperature

1 teaspoon vanilla extract

3 cups (390 g) all-purpose flour

1 tablespoon cornstarch

1½ teaspoons Diamond Crystal kosher salt

1 teaspoon baking soda

¾ cup (48 g) vanilla wafers (see Note)

¾ cup (128 g) white chocolate chips

¾ cup (32 g) mini marshmallows

1. Preheat the oven to 350°F (180°C). Line two baking sheets with parchment paper.
2. Place the brown sugar and butter in a large bowl. Use a stand mixer or hand mixer to mix until well combined, about 2 minutes.
3. Add the banana, pudding mix, eggs, and vanilla extract. Mix until combined and lighter in color, about 2 minutes.
4. Add the flour, cornstarch, salt, and baking soda. Mix on low until just combined, about 30 seconds.
5. Break the vanilla wafers into smaller pieces (but not crumbs). Add the wafers, white chocolate chips, and marshmallows. Mix on low until evenly distributed.
6. Use a large (4-tablespoon/2-ounce) cookie scoop to scoop the dough into balls. Place up to five balls onto each baking sheet, spaced equally apart.
7. Bake for 9 to 13 minutes, until the cookies are just starting to brown. Let the cookies cool for 10 minutes and then transfer to a cooling rack.
8. Repeat steps 6 and 7 to bake the remaining dough.

NOTE

Use vanilla wafers, such as Nilla Wafers, not cream-filled ones.

RICE KRISPIES TREAT COOKIES

This cookie will absolutely change how you look at Rice Krispies Treats. The brittle has the perfect caramelly bite while still preserving the delicate crunch of the Rice Krispies cereal it envelops. The brittle is added to a soft, chewy cookie studded with marshmallow fluff, creating a beautiful contrast of crunchy and soft. Basically the grown-up version of Rice Krispies Treats, this cookie will make you nostalgic for the original, but you'll never go back.

MAKES 9 LARGE COOKIES

Brown Butter

½ cup (113 g) salted butter, cubed

1 small ice cube

Rice Krispies Brittle (see Note 1; page 164)

¾ cup (150 g) granulated sugar

3 tablespoons salted butter

3 tablespoons water

1½ cups (40 g) Rice Krispies cereal

½ teaspoon baking soda

½ teaspoon Diamond Crystal kosher salt

Cookies

½ cup (108 g) brown sugar

¼ cup (50 g) granulated sugar

1 large egg, room temperature

1 teaspoon vanilla extract

1¼ cups (162 g) all-purpose flour

½ teaspoon baking soda

½ teaspoon Diamond Crystal kosher salt

½ cup (43 g) marshmallow fluff (see Note 2; page 164)

1. Make the brown butter: Heat a large pan over medium heat. Add the butter and stir until melted, about 1 minute. Keep stirring as the melted butter starts to bubble and then foam, about 2 minutes. After the foam subsides, you'll see brown flecks on the bottom of the pan, and the butter will smell very nutty. Pour the brown butter into a large heat-safe bowl, add the ice cube, and stir until the ice cube melts. Let the butter cool to room temperature. (If you are in a hurry, cover the bowl with plastic wrap or a lid and transfer to the fridge or freezer to speed up the process.)
2. Make the brittle: Line a baking sheet with parchment paper. Place the sugar, butter, and water in a medium pot over medium heat. Stir continually while the butter starts to melt, about 2 minutes. When the mixture starts to bubble, about 2 more minutes, stop actively stirring.
3. Continue to cook, swirling the pot every minute to gently stir, until the sugar turns a light brown color, about 5 minutes. Turn off the heat. Add the Rice Krispies, stirring constantly until completely coated, and then quickly stir in the baking soda and salt.
4. Carefully pour the hot mixture onto the baking sheet. Use the back of a spoon to spread the brittle into a thin layer and set aside to cool completely.
5. Make the cookies: Preheat the oven to 350°F (180°C). Line two baking sheets with parchment paper.

recipe continues...

NOTES

1. This recipe makes more brittle than you need. Save it to snack on or add it to other cookies! Store in an airtight container at room temperature for up to 10 days.

2. If you can't find marshmallow fluff, you can use mini marshmallows instead, but your cookies won't be as ooey-gooey.

6. Add the brown sugar and granulated sugar to the large bowl with the brown butter. Use a stand mixer or hand mixer to mix until combined, about 2 minutes.
7. Add the egg and vanilla extract and mix until combined, about 1 minute.
8. Add the flour, baking soda, and salt and mix until just combined, about 30 seconds.
9. Use a rolling pin or the back of a spoon to carefully break the cooled brittle into smaller pieces. Add a heaping ½ cup (80 g) of the brittle to the dough and mix until just combined.
10. Use two spoons to carefully spread dollops of marshmallow fluff across the top of the dough. Use a large (4-tablespoon/2-ounce) cookie scoop to scoop the dough into balls, making sure to get some marshmallow fluff in each scoop.
11. Place up to five dough balls onto each baking sheet, spaced equally apart. Press an extra piece of Rice Krispies brittle on top of each dough ball. Bake for 7 to 9 minutes, until the cookies are just set.
12. The marshmallow fluff will likely cause the cookies to come out irregularly shaped. Swirl a round cookie cutter around the cookies to bring all the rough edges in. Let the cookies cool on the baking sheets for 5 minutes and then transfer to a cooling rack to cool completely.

LEMON TART COOKIES

I never got to meet Connor's grandma, as she passed long before Connor and I even met, but I've pieced together my understanding of her through pictures and stories. She was a 4'10" Japanese woman who survived the internment camps of World War II, she often gave in to seven-year-old Connor's relentless pleas to buy him Pokémon cards, and she loved all things lemon. I like to imagine I'm making these cookies for her. These soft sugar cookies are shaped like a pie crust, filled with a creamy lemon mixture, and topped with a dollop of mascarpone whipped cream. The tart filling contains lots of lemon juice, which pairs perfectly with the sweet cookie and the creamy whipped topping.

MAKES 10 LARGE COOKIES

Sugar Cookies

½ cup (113 g) salted butter, softened

¼ cup (56 g) cream cheese, softened

¾ cup (150 g) granulated sugar

⅓ cup (72 g) brown sugar

1 large egg, room temperature

1 teaspoon vanilla extract

1¾ cups (227 g) all-purpose flour

½ teaspoon baking powder

½ teaspoon baking soda

½ teaspoon Diamond Crystal kosher salt

Lemon Filling

2 cups (480 ml) heavy cream

2 tablespoons honey

Zest of 2 lemons (about 2 tablespoons)

½ cup (120 ml) lemon juice

1 teaspoon vanilla extract

Pinch of Diamond Crystal kosher salt

Mascarpone Whipped Cream

½ cup (110 g) mascarpone cheese

½ cup (120 ml) heavy cream

1 tablespoon granulated sugar

½ teaspoon vanilla extract

Pinch of Diamond Crystal kosher salt

1. Make the cookies: Line a large plate with parchment paper. Place the butter and cream cheese in a large bowl. Use a stand mixer or hand mixer to mix until fully combined, about 1 minute.
2. Add the granulated sugar and brown sugar. Mix until fully combined and smooth, about 2 minutes.
3. Add the egg and vanilla extract and mix until fluffy and lighter in color, about 1 minute.
4. Add the flour, baking powder, baking soda, and salt. Mix on low just until the flour is combined, about 30 seconds.
5. Use a large (4-tablespoon/2-ounce) cookie scoop to scoop the dough into balls. Place the dough balls onto the plate and transfer to the fridge to chill for 2 hours.
6. Preheat the oven to 350°F (180°C). Line two baking sheets with parchment paper.
7. Use your fingers to create a 1½-inch (4 cm) indent in each dough ball, leaving a ¼-inch (6 mm) border and making sure not to poke through the bottom (see Note 1; page 168).
8. Place up to five dough balls onto each baking sheet, spaced equally apart. Bake for 9 to 11 minutes, until the edges are just starting to set.
9. Immediately after removing the cookies from the oven, use the bottom of a glass or a measuring cup that is just smaller than the width of the cookies to press down on the center, creating what looks like a small pie crust.

recipe continues...

10. Make the filling: Place the heavy cream, honey, and lemon zest in a large pot over medium heat. Stir until the mixture comes to a boil, about 5 minutes. Let it boil, stirring occasionally, for 5 minutes. Turn off the heat and add the lemon juice, vanilla extract, and salt and stir to combine. The mixture will thicken but still be pourable.
11. Carefully pour the hot liquid into the indent of each cookie (see Note 2). Let the cookies and filling cool completely (placing them in the fridge can speed up the cooling process).
12. Make the whipped cream: Place the mascarpone, heavy cream, sugar, vanilla extract, and salt in a medium bowl. Use a stand mixer or hand mixer to mix until soft peaks form, about 5 minutes. Just before serving, top each cookie with a dollop of the whipped cream, about 2 tablespoons per cookie. Store any extra cookies in the fridge.

NOTES

1. The dough ball won't stay in this shape after baking, but the indent makes the cookie easier to shape.

2. The lemon filling can be added while the cookies are still hot.

STICKY TOFFEE PUDDING COOKIES

I had my first sticky toffee pudding at the ripe age of twenty-seven while in London, and after one bite, I was instantly mourning the previous twenty-six years of my life without it. It's such a delightful, soft, and moist cake packed with molasses and warm spices. One of the key elements of sticky toffee pudding is blended dates that have been softened with hot water. Too much water doesn't do well in cookies, so we add some blended dates here, plus a few tablespoons of molasses to boost the rich caramel flavor. For the full sticky toffee pudding experience, these cookies are best enjoyed warm!

MAKES 10 LARGE COOKIES

Toffee

½ cup (100 g) granulated sugar

2 tablespoons salted butter, room temperature

2 tablespoons water

Pinch of Diamond Crystal kosher salt

Sticky Toffee Pudding Cookies

6 Medjool dates, pitted

1 cup (240 ml) hot water

½ cup (113 g) salted butter, softened

⅓ cup (72 g) brown sugar

¼ cup (50 g) granulated sugar

2 tablespoons molasses

1 large egg, room temperature

1 teaspoon vanilla extract

2 cups (260 g) all-purpose flour

½ teaspoon baking powder

½ teaspoon baking soda

½ teaspoon ground cinnamon

½ teaspoon ground ginger

½ teaspoon Diamond Crystal kosher salt

¼ cup (45 g) turbinado sugar

1. Make the toffee: Line a baking sheet with parchment paper. Heat a medium heavy-bottomed pot over medium-low heat. Add the granulated sugar, butter, water, and salt. Stir with a wooden spoon to combine and continue to gently stir as the butter melts, about 3 minutes. Then, stop actively stirring. The mixture will start to bubble. Continue stirring occasionally, about once every 2 minutes, and let boil until it turns a medium-brown color and reaches 295°F to 305°F (146°C to 151°C) on a candy thermometer, 10 to 14 minutes.
2. Carefully pour the hot mixture onto the baking sheet and use the back of your spoon to spread it into a thin, even layer. Let cool completely and then use the back of a spoon to break it into small pieces.
3. Make the cookies: Preheat the oven to 350°F (180°C). Line two baking sheets with parchment paper.
4. Submerge the dates in the water in a medium bowl. Let the dates soften for at least 10 minutes.
5. Place the butter, brown sugar, granulated sugar, and molasses in a large bowl. Use a stand mixer or hand mixer to mix until fully combined, about 2 minutes.
6. Transfer the dates and ¼ cup (60 ml) of the water to a blender or food processor. Blend until mostly smooth (a few small chunks are fine), about 1 minute. Pour the mixture into the large bowl. Add the egg and vanilla extract and mix until combined, about 1 minute.

7. Add the flour, baking powder, baking soda, cinnamon, ginger, and salt. Mix on low just until the flour is combined, about 30 seconds. Let the dough sit for 10 minutes for the flour to fully hydrate and the dough to slightly thicken.
8. Add a heaping ½ cup (78 g) of the toffee bits to the dough. Mix on low until evenly distributed through the dough.
9. Pour the turbinado sugar into a small shallow bowl.
10. Use a large (4-tablespoon/2-ounce) cookie scoop to scoop the dough into balls. Drop each dough ball into the turbinado sugar and roll to coat. Top each dough ball with a piece of toffee, gently pressing each piece into the dough.
11. Place up to five dough balls onto each baking sheet, spaced equally apart. Bake for 9 to 11 minutes, until the edges are just set. Let the cookies cool on the baking sheets for 10 minutes and then transfer to a cooling rack. Enjoy while the cookies are cool enough to eat but still warm.
12. To reheat the cookies, microwave each cookie for 5 to 10 seconds, until warm.

Flour
Butter

COOKIES INSPIRED BY TV SHOWS AND MOVIES

This is the series that started it all for me. Back in 2020, when I was just getting into content creation and my accounts were still very small, I started a little series called "Cookies Inspired by TV Shows and Movies." First was Stranger Things *(an Eggo waffle cookie, of course) and then later a coffee cake cookie for* Gilmore Girls *(page 175). This entire series blew up and really put me on the map. I stopped the series after a while, but I've brought it back for this book. I've included some of my favorites from the original series as well as several new ones that I think you'll love.*

GILMORE GIRLS COFFEE CAKE COOKIES

This cookie is very near and dear to me. If you've ever made a cookie recipe from my website, it was likely this one. I originally shared it back in 2020 as part of a series called "Cookies Inspired by TV Shows and Movies," which continues in this chapter. This recipe is still the most popular cookie I've ever shared, with nearly 40 million views across social media. In nearly every episode of Gilmore Girls, *Rory and Lorelai Gilmore visit Luke's Diner for a cup of coffee or a meal. Inspired by the Gilmore girls' love of coffee, this coffee cake cookie was born. Like normal coffee cake, this cookie doesn't have any coffee in it; instead, it's meant to be enjoyed with a cup of coffee. Cozy up on the couch with these cookies in hand, and you'll be transported straight to Stars Hollow.*

MAKES 12 LARGE COOKIES

Cinnamon Cookies

1 cup (215 g) brown sugar

½ cup (113 g) salted butter, softened

½ cup (120 ml) neutral oil (vegetable or canola works best)

1 large egg, room temperature

1 teaspoon vanilla extract

2½ cups (325 g) all-purpose flour

2 teaspoons ground cinnamon

1 teaspoon Diamond Crystal kosher salt

½ teaspoon baking powder

½ teaspoon baking soda

Streusel

½ cup (65 g) all-purpose flour

¼ cup (56 g) salted butter, softened

¼ cup (54 g) brown sugar

½ teaspoon ground cinnamon

¼ teaspoon Diamond Crystal kosher salt

Icing

½ cup (56 g) powdered sugar

1 tablespoon milk

¼ teaspoon vanilla extract

1. Preheat the oven to 350°F (180°C). Line two baking sheets with parchment paper.
2. Make the cookies: Place the brown sugar, butter, and oil in a large bowl. Use a stand mixer or hand mixer to mix until creamy, about 2 minutes.
3. Add the egg and vanilla extract and mix until combined, about 1 minute.
4. Add the flour, cinnamon, salt, baking powder, and baking soda. Mix until just combined.
5. Make the streusel: Place the flour, butter, brown sugar, cinnamon, and salt in a medium bowl. Use your fingers or a rubber spatula to mix until a dough forms, about 1 minute. The mixture should stick together when squeezed into a ball but crumble when you run your fingers through it.
6. Use a large (4-tablespoon/2-ounce) cookie scoop to scoop the cookie dough into balls. Place up to six balls onto each baking sheet, spaced equally apart. Use the back of the cookie scoop to indent the top of each ball about ½ inch (1 cm) deep.
7. Crumble about 2 tablespoons of the streusel into the indent of each dough ball.
8. Bake for 10 to 12 minutes, until the edges are just starting to set. Let the cookies cool for 10 minutes on the baking sheets and then transfer to a cooling rack to cool completely.
9. Meanwhile, make the icing: Whisk the powdered sugar, milk, and vanilla extract in a small bowl until smooth, about 1 minute. Drizzle icing on top of each cooled cookie.

HARRY POTTER BUTTERBEER SORTING HAT COOKIES

If you're anything like me, the first time you read or watched Harry Potter, *you wanted nothing more than to sit under the Sorting Hat and see which Hogwarts house you belonged to (I'm a Hufflepuff). Yes, there are online sorting hat quizzes galore, but let me introduce you to my favorite Sorting Hat method: cookies. These cookies are butterbeer flavored (thanks to the butterscotch pudding mix), and each one is stuffed with one color of M&M's: red for Gryffindor, blue for Ravenclaw, yellow for Hufflepuff, or green for Slytherin. You can't see the color from the outside, so pick whichever cookie is calling to you, break it in half, and reveal the house you belong to! It's almost as good as the real thing, plus you get a delicious cookie to eat afterward, so it might even be better.*

MAKES 16 LARGE COOKIES

1 cup (227 g) salted butter, softened

1 cup (215 g) brown sugar

½ cup (100 g) granulated sugar

One 3.4-ounce (96 g) box instant butterscotch pudding mix (see Note)

2 large eggs, room temperature

1 teaspoon vanilla extract

2¾ cups (358 g) all-purpose flour

1 teaspoon baking soda

1 teaspoon cornstarch

1 teaspoon Diamond Crystal kosher salt

1 cup (170 g) white chocolate chips

½ cup (100 g) red, blue, yellow, and green M&M's

1. Preheat the oven to 350°F (180°C). Line two baking sheets with parchment paper.
2. Place the butter, brown sugar, and granulated sugar in a large bowl. Use a stand mixer or hand mixer to mix until creamy, about 2 minutes.
3. Add the pudding mix, eggs, and vanilla extract. Mix until combined, about 1 minute.
4. Add the flour, baking soda, cornstarch, and salt. Mix on low until just combined, about 1 minute.
5. Add the white chocolate chips and mix on low until evenly distributed through the dough.
6. Use a large (4-tablespoon/2-ounce) cookie scoop to scoop the dough into balls. With the dough still in the scoop, use your fingers to make an indent in the dough. Add three to five M&M's of the same color to the center and then close the dough around the M&M's, making sure it's completely sealed. Repeat with the remaining dough, alternating among each of the four M&M colors.
7. Place up to six dough balls onto each baking sheet, spaced equally apart. Bake for 10 to 12 minutes, until the edges are just set. Let the cookies cool on the baking sheets for 10 minutes and then transfer to a cooling rack to cool completely.
8. Repeat steps 6 and 7 to bake the remaining dough.
9. Once the cookies have cooled, randomly pick a cookie to reveal your Hogwarts house.

NOTE

If you can't find butterscotch pudding mix, use salted caramel or vanilla pudding mix. The cookies won't have the distinctive butterbeer flavor, but they will still be delicious.

TED LASSO SHORTBREAD COOKIES

Ted Lasso *stole our hearts with its warm, happy story, but it also stole our stomachs with its ever-present shortbread cookies in an iconic pink box. Ted, an American football coach newly hired to coach soccer in England, always brings a batch to Rebecca, his new boss, and they quickly bring her onto his side. These cookies will undoubtedly have the same effect on anyone in your life. They are buttery, flaky, and not too sweet, like any good shortbread should be. You can cut them into whatever size you want, so they can fit into a little pink box, too.*

MAKES 16 COOKIES

1 cup (227 g) salted butter, softened

½ cup (100 g) granulated sugar

1 teaspoon vanilla extract

2 cups (260 g) all-purpose flour

½ teaspoon Diamond Crystal kosher salt

2 tablespoons turbinado sugar, optional (see Note)

1. Preheat the oven to 325°F (165°C). Line an 8-inch (20 cm) square baking pan with parchment paper.
2. Place the butter, sugar, and vanilla extract in a large bowl. Use a spoon or rubber spatula to mix until well combined and smooth, about 3 minutes.
3. Add the flour and salt. Mix until a dough forms and the flour is just combined, about 30 seconds.
4. Transfer the dough to the baking pan and use your hands, a rubber spatula, or a bench scraper to flatten it evenly.
5. Bake for 30 to 40 minutes, until the edges are starting to brown and the middle is just set.
6. Immediately after removing the cookies from the oven, sprinkle the turbinado sugar on top. Let the cookies cool in the pan for at least 20 minutes.
7. Lift the cookies out with the parchment paper and transfer to a cutting board. Use a large knife to cut the slab in half and then cut each half into eight 1-inch-wide (2.5 cm) rectangles.

NOTE

The turbinado sugar is optional, but it really brings a lot to these cookies. It adds a beautiful crunch on top, so try not to skip it!

THE PARENT TRAP PEANUT BUTTER OREOS

The Parent Trap *is undoubtedly the movie that defined my adolescence, the movie I watched over and over. Hallie and Annie, the movie's twin protagonists, were the definition of cool, and I obviously wanted to be them. And there is nothing more iconic than the moment that Hallie and Annie discover they both love Oreos dipped in peanut butter. As an ode to that moment, this recipe makes Oreo cookies but replaces the cream filling with a smooth and creamy peanut butter filling. The result is the perfect peanut butter Oreo cookie that our* Parent Trap *queens would be obsessed with. So, make these, take a bite, pierce your own ears, play a round of poker, and find your long-lost twin sister. Or maybe just eat them while you rewatch* The Parent Trap *for the millionth time!*

MAKES 20 SMALL COOKIE SANDWICHES

Oreo Cookies

One 15-ounce (425 g) box chocolate cake mix

¼ cup (56 g) salted butter, melted

2 large eggs, room temperature

1 tablespoon sour cream or plain Greek yogurt

Peanut Butter Filling

½ cup (135 g) creamy peanut butter (see Note)

¼ cup (56 g) salted butter, softened

½ teaspoon vanilla extract

¼ teaspoon Diamond Crystal kosher salt

2 cups (227 g) powdered sugar

1 to 2 tablespoons milk

1. Preheat the oven to 350°F (180°C). Line two baking sheets with parchment paper.
2. Make the cookies: Place the cake mix, butter, eggs, and sour cream in a large bowl. Using a stand or hand mixer, mix to form a sticky dough, about 1 minute.
3. Use a small (1-tablespoon/½-ounce) cookie scoop to scoop the dough into balls. Place up to ten balls onto each baking sheet, spaced equally apart. Bake for 8 to 11 minutes, until the middles are just set. Let the cookies cool on the baking sheets for 10 minutes and then transfer to a cooling rack. Repeat to bake the remaining dough.
4. Make the filling: Using a stand mixer or hand mixer, mix the peanut butter and butter in a medium bowl until creamy, about 2 minutes. Mix in the vanilla and salt. Mix in the powdered sugar and 1 tablespoon milk until smooth. If the frosting is too thick, add another tablespoon of milk.
5. Flip half of the cookies over. Pipe or spread about 1 tablespoon of the filling onto the flipped cookies and sandwich with the remaining cookies.

NOTE

Don't use natural peanut butter: Use Skippy, Jif, or another processed peanut butter.

BLUEY MINI PAVLOVAS

Bluey *is a popular Australian TV show that has quickly become a favorite of my daughter, Emi, and one of my favorites as well. In one episode, Bluey and her little sister, Bingo, do everything they can to score a slice of pavlova from their fridge while their dad, Bandit, tries to convince them to eat edamame beans instead (spoiler: the kids prevail). Pavlova is a baked meringue dessert that is very popular in Australia, especially at Christmastime. It's usually topped with whipped cream and fruit, often with some kind of curd. Here, we're making mini pavlovas with a cookie twist. Each mini pavlova is topped with the typical whipped cream and fruit, but we also add a brown sugar shortbread crumble, which provides a delightful texture. Plus, these mini pavlovas are the perfect size—small enough for Bluey and Bingo to each enjoy their own, unless they choose edamame beans this time.*

MAKES 16 MINI PAVLOVAS

Mini Pavlovas

1 cup (200 g) granulated sugar

1 tablespoon cornstarch

4 large egg whites, room temperature

1 teaspoon cream of tartar

Cookie Crumble

½ cup (113 g) salted butter, softened

¼ cup (54 g) brown sugar

½ teaspoon vanilla extract

1 cup (130 g) all-purpose flour

¼ teaspoon Diamond Crystal kosher salt

Toppings (see Note)

1 cup (240 ml) heavy cream

1 tablespoon granulated sugar

2 cups (240 g) fresh raspberries

NOTE

Add whatever toppings you'd like: If you prefer a different fruit, go for it. You could also add any sort of jam or curd. Make it your own!

1. Preheat the oven to 250°F (120°C). Line two baking sheets and an 8-inch (20 cm) square baking pan with parchment paper.
2. Make the pavlovas: Combine the sugar and cornstarch in a small bowl.
3. Place the egg whites in a large bowl. Use a stand mixer or hand mixer to mix until the eggs are frothy, about 3 minutes, and then add the cream of tartar. Continue to mix until stiff peaks form, about 3 more minutes.
4. With the mixer still on, add 1 tablespoon of the sugar mixture at a time, mixing for 30 seconds between each addition.
5. Rub some of the meringue through your fingers to see if you can feel any grains of sugar. If you can, continue to mix until you cannot feel the sugar anymore.
6. Using a large (4-tablespoon/2-ounce) cookie scoop, scoop the meringue onto the baking sheets in individual mounds. Scoop up to eight mounds onto each baking sheet, spaced equally apart. Use the back of a spoon to make a 1-inch-deep (2.5 cm) indent into each mound.
7. Bake for 60 to 90 minutes, until the pavlovas are no longer sticky and are hard to the touch. Leave the pavlovas in the oven, turn it off, and prop open the door to allow the pavlovas to cool down slowly for about 2 hours.

recipe continues...

8. Remove the pavlovas from the oven and then preheat the oven to 350°F (180°C).
9. Make the crumble: Place the butter, brown sugar, and vanilla extract in a large bowl. Use a stand mixer or hand mixer to mix until fully combined, about 2 minutes.
10. Add the flour and salt. Mix on low just until the flour is combined, about 15 seconds.
11. Transfer the dough to the baking pan. Use your fingers to press the dough into the pan until it is evenly spread out. Bake for 10 minutes and then drag a fork through the cookie to break it into ½-inch (1 cm) crumbles. The cookie will still look quite doughy at this point. Bake for an additional 10 to 15 minutes, until the crumbles are golden brown and cooked through, using a fork to crumble the dough every 5 minutes. Let the crumble cool completely.
12. Make the toppings: Place the heavy cream and sugar in a large bowl. Use a hand mixer or a stand mixer with a whisk attachment to whip until soft peaks form, 4 to 6 minutes.
13. To assemble, add a dollop of whipped cream on top of each pavlova and then a few raspberries, followed by a generous handful of cookie crumble.

STAR WARS WOOKIEE WHOOPIE PIES

I watched all the original Star Wars *movies for the first time when I was eleven years old on a six-inch TV that was attached to the ceiling of my parents' minivan. We were on a long family road trip, and my three older brothers decided a* Star Wars *marathon was the move, even though I was skeptical. I know I missed a few plot points thanks to the tiny screen and some naps here and there, but I was surprised by how much I thoroughly enjoyed each movie. These cookies are a nod to several of the best parts of* Star Wars*: Wookiees, a species of giant hairy aliens (whoopie pie); the light side of the Force (vanilla cake); the dark side of the Force (chocolate cake); and the* Star Wars *galaxy (colored frosting).*

MAKES 18 MEDIUM COOKIE SANDWICHES

Wookiee Whoopie Pie Cakes

1 cup (215 g) brown sugar

½ cup (113 g) salted butter, softened

1 large egg, room temperature

1 teaspoon vanilla extract

2¼ cups (292 g) plus 1 tablespoon all-purpose flour, divided

1 teaspoon baking soda

½ teaspoon Diamond Crystal kosher salt

1 cup plus 1½ tablespoons (260 ml) buttermilk, room temperature, divided

3 tablespoons cocoa powder

Galaxy Frosting

4 ounces (113 g) cream cheese, softened

¼ cup (56 g) salted butter, softened

2 cups (227 g) powdered sugar

1 teaspoon vanilla extract

Black, blue, and purple food coloring

1. Preheat the oven to 350°F (180°C). Line two baking sheets with parchment paper.
2. Make the cakes: Place the brown sugar and butter in a large bowl. Use a stand mixer or hand mixer to mix until combined, about 2 minutes.
3. Add the egg and vanilla extract and mix until combined, about 1 minute.
4. Place 2¼ cups (292 g) flour, the baking soda, and the salt in a small bowl. Mix until combined.
5. Add about half of the buttermilk to the large bowl and mix until combined, about 15 seconds. Add about half of the flour mixture and mix just until no streaks of flour remain, about 15 seconds. Repeat with the remaining buttermilk and flour.
6. Pour half of the batter into a separate medium bowl. Add the remaining 1 tablespoon of flour to the large bowl and mix until just combined. Add the cocoa powder to the medium bowl and mix until just combined.
7. Use a medium (2-tablespoon/1-ounce) cookie scoop to scoop the vanilla dough into balls. Place up to 12 dough balls, spaced equally apart, onto one baking sheet.
8. Repeat step 7 with the chocolate dough and the other baking sheet. Bake for 10 to 13 minutes, until the edges are just set. Let the cookies cool on the baking sheets for 10 minutes and then transfer to a cooling rack to cool completely.
9. Repeat steps 7 and 8 with the remaining dough.

recipe continues...

10. Make the frosting: Place the cream cheese and butter in a medium bowl. Use a hand mixer or stand mixer to mix until well combined, about 1 minute. Add the powdered sugar and vanilla extract and mix until smooth, about 1 minute.
11. Divide the frosting into three small bowls. Add a few drops of black food coloring to the first bowl, a few drops of blue food coloring to the second bowl, and a few drops of purple food coloring to the third bowl. Stir each to combine, about 1 minute.
12. Place a large piece of plastic wrap on the counter. Working with one color at a time, use a spoon or rubber spatula to scoop the frosting onto the plastic wrap in long rows, about 12 inches (30 cm) long. Place the next color directly above the first so the two colors are touching. Repeat with the remaining color. Starting at one of the long sides, roll the plastic wrap into a log shape. Twist the ends of the plastic wrap and cut one of the ends off just before the frosting.
13. Slide the log into a piping bag. Flip over all the vanilla cookies. Pipe 1 to 2 tablespoons of frosting onto each vanilla cookie and sandwich each with a chocolate cookie, gently pressing them together to adhere. Store any extra cookies in the fridge.

Mints
PRODUCT SOLD BY WEIGHT NOT VOLUME.
CONTENTS TEND TO SETTLE AFTER PACKAGING.
Junior Mints

SEINFELD JUNIOR MINT COOKIES

Seinfeld *has endless iconic moments, so figuring out the theme of this cookie was a hard one. But I ultimately decided I wanted to pay homage to my favorite character, Kramer, Jerry Seinfeld's wacky next-door neighbor. He has many unforgettable scenes, but arguably his most well-known moment comes in the "Junior Mint" episode. Kramer and Jerry are watching a surgery being performed on their friend, and Kramer pops out a box of Junior Mints to snack on. Jerry starts to protest, telling him to put them away, and in the struggle, one Junior Mint gets loose and flies into the surgical area, lodging in the patient. Just like in this iconic moment, we're stuffing each cookie with one singular Junior Mint and then wrapping the dough around it. Lucky for all of us, these cookies actually benefit from having a Junior Mint inside.*

MAKES 8 LARGE COOKIES

½ cup (113 g) salted butter, softened

½ cup (108 g) brown sugar

⅓ cup (66 g) granulated sugar

1 large egg, room temperature

1 teaspoon vanilla extract

1½ cups (195 g) all-purpose flour

1 teaspoon baking powder

½ teaspoon Diamond Crystal kosher salt

½ cup (65 g) roughly chopped Andes Mints

8 Junior Mints

1. Preheat the oven to 350°F (180°C). Line two baking sheets with parchment paper.
2. Place the butter, brown sugar, and granulated sugar in a large bowl. Use a stand mixer or hand mixer to mix until fully combined, about 2 minutes.
3. Add the egg and vanilla extract and mix until fluffy and lighter in color, about 1 minute.
4. Add the flour, baking powder, and salt. Mix on low just until the flour is combined, about 30 seconds.
5. Add the Andes Mints to the dough, reserving a handful of pieces for topping, and mix on low until evenly distributed through the dough.
6. Use a large (4-tablespoon/2-ounce) cookie scoop to scoop the dough into balls. With the dough still in the cookie scoop, push one Junior Mint into the center of each dough ball and then securely close the dough around it. Place up to four dough balls onto each baking sheet, spaced equally apart.
7. Bake for 10 to 12 minutes, until the edges are just set. Press some reserved pieces of Andes Mint on top of each cookie. Let the cookies cool on the baking sheets for 10 minutes and then transfer to a cooling rack to cool completely.

PARKS AND REC WAFFLE COOKIES

Anyone who has watched even a few episodes of Parks and Recreation *knows how obsessed the main character, Leslie, is with waffles. Any chance she can get, she is at a diner eating a large stack with plenty of butter and maple syrup. These cookies are an ode to Leslie, with a maple syrup dough and a generous dollop of buttercream on top. I highly recommend stacking a few on a plate, adding the buttercream and an extra drizzle of maple syrup, and eating them with a fork and knife. It's the way Leslie would want it.*

MAKES 10 LARGE COOKIES

Maple Cookies

1 cup (215 g) brown sugar

½ cup (90 g) vegetable shortening

¼ cup (56 g) salted butter, softened

1 large egg, room temperature

2 tablespoons maple syrup

2 cups (260 g) all-purpose flour

1 tablespoon cornstarch

½ teaspoon baking soda

½ teaspoon Diamond Crystal kosher salt

Buttercream Frosting

1 cup (113 g) powdered sugar

¼ cup (56 g) salted butter, softened

½ teaspoon vanilla extract

1. Preheat the oven to 350°F (180°C). Line two baking sheets with parchment paper.
2. Make the cookies: Place the brown sugar, shortening, and butter in a large bowl. Use a stand or hand mixer to mix until fully combined, about 2 minutes. Add the egg and maple syrup and mix until fluffy and lighter in color, about 1 minute.
3. Add the flour, cornstarch, baking soda, and salt. Mix on low just until the flour is combined, about 30 seconds.
4. Using a large (4-tablespoon/2-ounce) cookie scoop, scoop the dough into balls. Place up to five balls onto each baking sheet, spaced equally apart. Use a skewer or chopstick to create a crosshatch on the top of each cookie.
5. Bake for 10 to 12 minutes, until the edges are just set. If the crosshatch becomes less defined, use the skewer or chopstick to redefine the lines right after the cookies finish baking. Let the cookies cool on the baking sheets for 10 minutes and then transfer to a cooling rack to cool completely.
6. Make the frosting: Place the powdered sugar, butter, and vanilla extract in a medium bowl. Use a hand mixer to mix until smooth, about 2 minutes. Use a small (1-tablespoon/½-ounce) cookie scoop to scoop a ball of frosting on top of each cooled cookie.

SURVIVOR COCONUT IMMUNITY COOKIES

First airing in 2000 and releasing two seasons each year, Survivor *has solidified itself in TV history. In the show, players are left on the beautiful beaches of Fiji to fend for themselves and their tribes with barely any food. They often survive off of the coconuts they find, plus fish when they can catch them. One of the most iconic elements of* Survivor *is the immunity idols. If a contestant finds an idol hidden on the beach or in the jungle, they can play it at tribal council and guarantee their safety. This* Survivor *cookie is an ode to many of these elements. A soft "sand" cookie is stuffed with a freeze-dried strawberry (aka an immunity idol) and then topped with a smooth coconut frosting. You can fill each cookie with an immunity idol, or you can just hide one so that whoever bites into that cookie is safe.*

MAKES 8 LARGE COOKIES

Sand Cookies

10 Golden Oreos

⅔ cup (144 g) brown sugar

½ cup (113 g) salted butter, softened

1 large egg, room temperature

1 teaspoon vanilla extract

1¼ cups (162 g) all-purpose flour

1 tablespoon cornstarch

½ teaspoon baking powder

½ teaspoon Diamond Crystal kosher salt

8 freeze-dried strawberry pieces

Coconut Frosting

One 3.4-ounce (96 g) box instant coconut pudding mix (see Note)

1 cup (240 ml) milk

1 cup (240 ml) heavy cream

1 teaspoon vanilla extract

2 tablespoons shredded coconut, optional

NOTE

If you can't find coconut-flavored pudding, vanilla will work just fine.

1. Preheat the oven to 350°F (180°C). Line two baking sheets with parchment paper.
2. Make the cookies: Pull the Oreos apart and scrape off the cream filling. Transfer the cookies to a food processor and blend to form crumbs, about 1 minute.
3. Place the brown sugar and butter in a large bowl. Use a stand mixer or hand mixer to mix until fully combined, about 2 minutes.
4. Add the egg and vanilla extract and mix until fluffy and lighter in color, about 1 minute.
5. Add the flour, ½ cup (50 g) of the Oreo crumbs, and the cornstarch, baking powder, and salt. Mix on low just until the flour is combined, about 30 seconds.
6. Use a large (4-tablespoon/2-ounce) cookie scoop to scoop the dough into balls. With the dough still in the cookie scoop, push one piece of freeze-dried strawberry into the center of each dough ball and then securely close the dough around it.
7. Place the remaining Oreo crumbs in a shallow bowl. Roll each dough ball in the palms of your hands until smooth and then drop it into the Oreo crumbs and roll to coat.

8. Place up to four dough balls onto each baking sheet, spaced equally apart. Bake for 10 to 12 minutes, until the edges are just set. Let the cookies cool on the baking sheets for 10 minutes and then transfer to a cooling rack to cool completely.
9. Meanwhile, make the frosting: Place the pudding mix and milk in a medium bowl. Whisk until smooth, about 1 minute. Cover with plastic wrap and transfer to the fridge to set up for at least 20 minutes.
10. Place the heavy cream and vanilla extract in a large bowl. Use a hand mixer or stand mixer to mix until stiff peaks form, 4 to 6 minutes. Transfer half of the whipped cream to the bowl with the pudding mix. Gently fold to combine, about 1 minute. Add the remaining whipped cream and fold until combined and smooth, about 1 minute.
11. When the cookies are completely cool, use a piping bag to pipe 2 to 3 tablespoons of frosting onto each cookie. Top each cookie with a pinch of shredded coconut, if using. Store any extra cookies in the fridge.

CLUELESS CHECKERBOARD SHORTBREAD COOKIES

Few things are more instantly recognizable than Cher's yellow plaid outfit from the movie Clueless. *Cher, a self-proclaimed matchmaker, serves looks in every scene as she tries to fix everyone else's life before realizing her own might need a little recalibrating. I made these checkerboard shortbread cookies in honor of the incredible yellow plaid blazer and miniskirt Cher sports at the beginning of the film. Vanilla and chocolate shortbreads are cut and layered into a checkerboard shape, making these cookies almost too pretty to eat—but after you experience their flaky texture and buttery taste, you'll be glad you did.*

MAKES 18 SMALL COOKIES

½ cup (113 g) salted butter, cold and cubed

½ cup (100 g) granulated sugar

1 large egg yolk

½ teaspoon vanilla extract

1½ cups (195 g) all-purpose flour

¼ teaspoon Diamond Crystal kosher salt

1½ tablespoons cold water

1 tablespoon cocoa powder

¼ cup (45 g) turbinado sugar, optional

1. Place the butter and sugar in a large bowl. Use a stand mixer or hand mixer to mix until combined, about 2 minutes.
2. Add the egg yolk and vanilla extract and mix until combined, about 1 minute.
3. Add the flour and salt. Mix on low until a crumbly dough forms, about 30 seconds. With the mixer on low, slowly add the water and mix just until a soft, cohesive dough forms.
4. Remove half of the dough (about ¾ cup/190 g) and place in a small bowl. Add the cocoa powder to the dough still in the mixer and mix on low just until combined, about 30 seconds.
5. Shape each half of the dough into a square. Wrap both in plastic wrap and transfer to the fridge to chill for 30 minutes.
6. Preheat the oven to 350°F (180°C). Line two baking sheets with parchment paper.
7. Remove the chilled dough from the fridge. Carefully roll out each dough ball into a 5-inch-wide (13 cm), ¼-inch-thick (6 mm) square. The dough will be very cold. Be patient, and the dough will start to work with you. Try to make the two squares as similar in shape as you can.
8. Stack the dough squares on top of each other, gently pressing down to adhere the two pieces together. Cut the stacked dough in half and then stack one half on top of the other, making sure the colors are alternating. Wrap with plastic wrap and transfer to the fridge to chill for 10 minutes.

recipe continues...

9. Remove the dough from the fridge and use a sharp knife to cut the dough lengthwise into ¼-inch-thick (6 mm) slices.
10. Bring one slice in front of you, laid flat, so you can see all the alternating colors. Grab another slice and stack it on top, making sure the colors are alternating. (If the vanilla dough is on the left, the piece going on top should have the chocolate dough on the left.) Gently press down to adhere the two pieces together. Repeat with two more pieces so you have four total pieces stacked, making sure the colors are alternating with each piece.
11. Cut off the rough ends, revealing a checkerboard pattern. Sprinkle each side of the stacked dough with turbinado sugar, if using, and press gently to adhere.
12. Slice the rectangular log of dough into ¼-inch-thick (6 mm) slices. Place up to twelve slices onto each baking sheet, spaced equally apart.
13. Bake for 7 to 9 minutes, just until the cookies stop looking doughy. Let the cookies cool on the baking sheets for 10 minutes and then transfer to a cooling rack to cool completely.

SMALL-BATCH COOKIES

Sometimes (more often than not), you want a cookie and you want it now. But you can't be bothered to pull out every bowl and pan in your house to make a full batch. Enter these small-batch cookies. Most recipes make two large cookies and come together in one bowl, no mixer required. You can have these cookies in your mouth stat, and you don't have to figure out what to do with the eight extra cookies from a typical batch. Whether you're baking just for yourself (baking is the best form of self-love) or for you and someone else, these recipes are perfect.

SMALL-BATCH BROWN BUTTER CCC

As we have established in my Brown Butter CCC recipe on page 60, brown butter chocolate chip cookies have my heart. So, obviously, we need them in small-batch form, too, so we can have them on a whim. This small batch makes two large cookies, and the whole thing can be mixed by hand in a small bowl. These BB CCCs are thick, but not too thick, with the perfect soft bite. Eat them both yourself, or share with someone else and win over their heart forever.

MAKES 2 LARGE COOKIES

¼ cup (56 g) salted butter, cubed
¼ cup (54 g) brown sugar
2 tablespoons granulated sugar
1 large egg yolk, room temperature
½ teaspoon vanilla extract
½ cup (65 g) all-purpose flour
¼ teaspoon baking soda
¼ teaspoon Diamond Crystal kosher salt
¼ cup (42 g) chocolate chunks (milk, semisweet, dark, or a mix), plus extra for topping
Flaky salt, for topping

1. Heat a medium pan over medium heat. Add the butter and stir until melted, about 2 minutes. Keep stirring as the melted butter starts to bubble and then foam, 3 to 5 minutes. After the foam subsides, you'll see brown flecks on the bottom of the pan, and the butter will smell very nutty. Pour the brown butter into a medium heat-safe bowl and then transfer to the freezer to chill for about 10 minutes, until the butter has cooled to the touch.
2. Preheat the oven to 350°F (180°C). Line a baking sheet with parchment paper.
3. Add the brown sugar and granulated sugar to the bowl with the brown butter. Whisk until combined, about 1 minute.
4. Add the egg yolk and vanilla extract and mix until smooth and glossy, about 1 minute.
5. Add the flour, baking soda, and kosher salt. Use a rubber spatula to mix until just combined, about 1 minute.
6. Add the chocolate chunks and mix until evenly distributed throughout the dough.
7. Use your hands to divide the dough in half and gently shape each half into a ball. Place both dough balls on the baking sheet, spaced equally apart, and top each dough ball with a chocolate chunk.
8. Bake for 8 to 10 minutes, until the edges are starting to brown. Top each cookie with a pinch of flaky salt. Let the cookies cool on the baking sheet for 5 minutes and then transfer to a cooling rack to cool completely.

SMALL-BATCH BAKERY-STYLE CCC

Put a finger down if you've ever walked into a bakery, seen a beautiful, thick chocolate chip cookie, and purchased it immediately, just to take a bite and realize it was dry and tough. I tragically have multiple fingers down, and I'm guessing you do, too. But don't be too sad, because this bakery-style CCC is here to fix all of our problems. It looks just as stunning as those gorgeous, thick cookies you see in a bakery but is soft and gooey. This small-batch recipe makes two cookies, perfect for any late-night craving.

MAKES 2 LARGE COOKIES

¼ cup plus 2 tablespoons (80 g) brown sugar

¼ cup (56 g) butter, softened

1 large egg yolk, room temperature

½ teaspoon vanilla extract

½ cup (65 g) all-purpose flour

1 tablespoon cornstarch

¼ teaspoon baking soda

¼ teaspoon Diamond Crystal kosher salt

½ cup (85 g) semisweet chocolate chips

1. Whisk the brown sugar and butter in a large bowl until combined, about 1 minute.
2. Add the egg yolk and vanilla extract and mix until combined, about 1 minute.
3. Add the flour, cornstarch, baking soda, and salt. Use a rubber spatula to mix until just combined, about 1 minute.
4. Add the chocolate chips and mix to evenly distribute throughout the dough.
5. Use your hands to divide the dough in half and shape each half into a dough ball. Cover with plastic wrap and transfer to the freezer for 1 hour to chill.
6. When the dough has 15 minutes of chill time remaining, preheat the oven to 350°F (180°C). Line a baking sheet with parchment paper.
7. Transfer the dough balls to the baking sheet, spaced equally apart. Bake for 10 to 12 minutes, until the edges are just set. Let the cookies cool on the baking sheet for 10 minutes and then transfer to a cooling rack to cool completely (or dive in early if you want an ooey-gooey cookie).

SMALL-BATCH LEMON RASPBERRY COOKIES

Lemon and raspberry is one of the best combinations. Lemon zest is bright and fresh, and raspberries are slightly sweet and tart. The shared acidic tang harmonizes together, with neither fruit overpowering the other. These cookies also have white chocolate added in to bring in a touch more sweetness. The combination tastes like a burst of summer that can be enjoyed at any time of year! Since the raspberries in these cookies are fresh, I recommend just barely pressing them into the dough when you mix. We want to release as little of the juice as possible so the cookies don't get soggy.

MAKES 2 LARGE COOKIES

2 tablespoons granulated sugar

Zest of 1 lemon (about 1 tablespoon)

¼ cup (56 g) salted butter, softened

¼ cup (54 g) brown sugar

1 large egg yolk, room temperature

½ teaspoon vanilla extract

⅔ cup (86 g) all-purpose flour

½ teaspoon baking powder

½ teaspoon Diamond Crystal kosher salt

2 tablespoons white chocolate chips

4 or 5 fresh raspberries (see Note)

1. Preheat the oven to 350°F (180°C). Line a baking sheet with parchment paper.
2. Place the granulated sugar and lemon zest in a medium bowl. Use your fingers to rub the lemon zest into the sugar, releasing the lemon oil.
3. Add the butter and brown sugar. Use a hand mixer or rubber spatula to mix until well combined, about 1 minute.
4. Add the egg yolk and vanilla extract and mix until smooth, about 1 minute.
5. Add the flour, baking powder, and salt. Mix just until no streaks of flour remain, about 30 seconds.
6. Add the white chocolate chips and mix until just combined. Gently break the raspberries into smaller pieces and place them into the dough. Carefully mix until just combined, trying not to burst any of the raspberries.
7. Use your hands to divide the dough in half and shape each half into a smooth ball. Place both dough balls on the baking sheet, spaced equally apart.
8. Bake for 10 to 13 minutes, until the edges are set and starting to brown. Let the cookies cool on the baking sheet for 15 minutes and then transfer to a cooling rack to cool completely.

NOTE

Freeze-dried raspberries work, too!

SMALL-BATCH FUNFETTI COOKIES

I hear the experts are saying it's impossible to be sad with a Funfetti cookie in hand. Imagine how impossible that is with two extra-large Funfetti cookies in hand? You can practically feel all sadness leaving your body. And to make it even better? You only need one tiny bowl and a rubber spatula to make these cookies a reality. So, what are you waiting for?

MAKES 2 EXTRA-LARGE COOKIES

¼ cup (56 g) salted butter, softened

¼ cup (50 g) granulated sugar

2 tablespoons powdered sugar

1 tablespoon plain Greek yogurt, room temperature

½ teaspoon vanilla extract

⅔ cup (86 g) all-purpose flour

½ teaspoon baking soda

½ teaspoon Diamond Crystal kosher salt

¼ teaspoon baking powder

¼ cup (50 g) rainbow sprinkles (see Note)

1. Preheat the oven to 350°F (180°C). Line a baking sheet with parchment paper.
2. Place the butter, granulated sugar, and powdered sugar in a medium bowl. Use a rubber spatula to mix until combined, about 2 minutes.
3. Add the yogurt and vanilla extract and mix until combined, about 1 minute.
4. Add the flour, baking soda, salt, and baking powder. Mix until just combined with a few streaks of flour remaining, about 30 seconds.
5. Add the sprinkles and mix until just distributed throughout the dough with no streaks of flour remaining.
6. Use your hands to divide the dough in half and shape each half into a ball. Place both dough balls on the baking sheet, spaced equally apart.
7. Bake for 10 to 13 minutes, until the edges are just starting to set. Let the cookies cool on the baking sheet for 10 minutes and then transfer to a cooling rack to cool completely.

NOTE

Add different sprinkles for whatever occasion you're celebrating: Valentine's Day, Christmas, Halloween, birthdays, and more!

SMALL-BATCH SNICKERDOODLE COOKIES

Snickerdoodles are a humble cookie—no mix-ins, just soft dough coated in cinnamon sugar—but their simplicity is what makes them great. These are large and soft, yet slightly dense, and they stay soft thanks to the yogurt and lower baking temperature. With no mix-ins in the way, you can fully appreciate this cookie for exactly what it is.

MAKES 2 LARGE COOKIES

¼ cup (56 g) salted butter, softened

¼ cup (54 g) brown sugar

3 tablespoons granulated sugar, divided

2 tablespoons plain Greek yogurt (see Note)

½ teaspoon vanilla extract

¾ cup (98 g) all-purpose flour

1 teaspoon cornstarch

½ teaspoon Diamond Crystal kosher salt

¼ teaspoon baking soda

½ teaspoon ground cinnamon

1. Preheat the oven to 325°F (165°C). Line a baking sheet with parchment paper.
2. Place the butter, the brown sugar, and 2 tablespoons granulated sugar in a medium bowl. Use a rubber spatula to mix until combined, about 2 minutes.
3. Add the yogurt and vanilla extract and whisk until fully combined, about 1 minute.
4. Add the flour, cornstarch, salt, and baking soda. Mix until just combined with no streaks of flour remaining, about 1 minute.
5. Combine the remaining 1 tablespoon granulated sugar and the cinnamon in a small bowl.
6. Use your hands to divide the dough in half and shape each half into a ball. Roll one dough ball at a time in the cinnamon sugar to coat completely.
7. Place both dough balls on the baking sheet, spaced about 4 inches (10 cm) apart. Bake for 10 to 14 minutes, until the edges are just set and starting to crack.
8. Let the cookies cool on the baking sheet for 5 minutes and then transfer to a cooling rack to cool completely.

NOTE

If you don't have plain Greek yogurt, use sour cream instead.

SMALL-BATCH NO-BAKE COOKIES

Sometimes, I cannot be bothered to turn on my oven, but I can always be bothered to make a little sweet treat. These cookies are the perfect solution for those moments. No oven required, just a few simple ingredients, and you've got four oat-packed cookies that are perfectly chocolatey and peanut buttery with lots of flaky salt on top. They're rich and indulgent, so a small batch is all you need. And since they're filled with oats and peanut butter, they're healthy, right?

MAKES 4 LARGE COOKIES

¼ cup plus 2 tablespoons (80 g) brown sugar

2 tablespoons salted butter

2 tablespoons milk

1 tablespoon cocoa powder

¾ cup (68 g) rolled oats

4 tablespoons peanut butter (see Notes 1 and 2), divided

Splash of vanilla extract

Pinch of Diamond Crystal kosher salt

Flaky salt, for topping

1. Line a baking sheet or large plate with parchment paper.
2. Heat a large pan over medium heat. Add the brown sugar, butter, milk, and cocoa powder and stir to combine, about 1 minute. Continue to stir while the mixture comes to a slow boil.
3. Boil for 1 minute and then remove from the heat. Add the oats, 3 tablespoons peanut butter, the vanilla extract, and the kosher salt. Stir until well combined, about 1 minute.
4. Let the mixture cool for 5 minutes.
5. Use a large (4-tablespoon/2-ounce) cookie scoop to scoop the mixture into balls. Place the dough balls on the baking sheet or plate, spaced equally apart. The dough will still be warm and a bit runny. Transfer to the fridge and let set for at least 20 minutes.
6. Add the remaining tablespoon of peanut butter to a small microwave-safe bowl. Microwave for 15 to 20 seconds, until melted and smooth. Drizzle the warm peanut butter on top of each cookie and then top with a pinch of flaky salt.

NOTES

1. Non-natural peanut butter (like Jif or Skippy) works best for these cookies, but you can use natural peanut butter if you'd like. The dough will be a bit runnier, but just let it set for an extra 5 minutes in step 4, and you'll be good to go.

2. Allergic to peanut butter? No worries! Use any nut butter you'd like, or if you're allergic to all nuts, use sunflower butter or even Biscoff spread!

SMALL-BATCH SPECULOOS WHITE CHOCOLATE COOKIES

Speculoos cookies are a type of shortbread cookie that originated in Belgium. You've probably had many in your day as an airplane snack under the brand name Biscoff. To me, they taste like a cross between a gingersnap and a graham cracker, and they're crunchy and addicting. We're adding both speculoos cookies and speculoos spread to this recipe to really let them shine. And their spiced flavor pairs perfectly with white chocolate chips. This small batch makes two extra-large cookies and is the perfect late-night baking project.

MAKES 2 EXTRA-LARGE COOKIES

¼ cup (56 g) salted butter, melted
¼ cup (54 g) brown sugar
2 tablespoons granulated sugar
¼ cup (72 g) speculoos spread
1 large egg yolk, room temerature
½ teaspoon vanilla extract
⅔ cup (86 g) all-purpose flour
¼ teaspoon baking soda
¼ teaspoon Diamond Crystal kosher salt
¼ cup (42 g) white chocolate chips
¼ cup (20 g) crushed speculoos cookies, plus two chunks for topping

1. Preheat the oven to 350°F (180°C). Line a baking sheet with parchment paper.
2. Place the butter, brown sugar, and granulated sugar in a large bowl. Use a rubber spatula to mix until combined, about 1 minute.
3. Add the speculoos spread, egg yolk, and vanilla extract. Mix until combined, about 1 minute.
4. Add the flour, baking soda, and salt. Gently mix until no streaks of flour remain, about 1 minute.
5. Add the white chocolate chips and speculoos cookie chunks and gently mix until evenly distributed throughout the dough.
6. Use your hands to divide the dough in half and shape each half into a large ball. Place both balls on the baking sheet, spaced equally apart. Press a cookie chunk on top of each dough ball.
7. Bake for 12 to 15 minutes, until the edges are just starting to brown. Let the cookies cool on the baking sheet for 10 minutes and then transfer to a cooling rack to cool completely.

SMALL-BATCH BLACK SESAME AND TAHINI COOKIES

Like the Halva Black Sesame Cookies on page 109, these cookies are packed with sesame flavor. The tahini provides a sweet, nutty taste and almost sand-like texture, while the black sesame seeds on the outside of the cookie bring an ever-so-slight bitterness and an even nuttier flavor. The combination is delightful and surprisingly not overwhelmingly sesame. Even if you aren't sesame obsessed, you'll still love these cookies.

MAKES 2 EXTRA-LARGE COOKIES

¼ cup (56 g) salted butter, melted

3 tablespoons brown sugar

3 tablespoons granulated sugar

3 tablespoons tahini

1 large egg yolk, room temperature

½ cup plus 2 tablespoons (82 g) all-purpose flour

¼ teaspoon baking soda

¼ teaspoon Diamond Crystal kosher salt

1 tablespoon black sesame seeds

1. Preheat the oven to 350°F (180°C). Line a baking sheet with parchment paper.
2. Place the butter, brown sugar, and granulated sugar in a large bowl. Use a rubber spatula to mix until fully combined, about 1 minute.
3. Add the tahini and egg yolk. Mix until the egg yolk is emulsified and the mixture is smooth, about 30 seconds.
4. Add the flour, baking soda, and salt. Mix just until no streaks of flour remain, about 30 seconds.
5. Use your hands to divide the dough in half and shape each half into a large ball.
6. Place the sesame seeds in a shallow bowl. Roll one dough ball at a time in the sesame seeds to coat completely.
7. Place each dough ball on the baking sheet, spaced equally apart. Bake for 11 to 14 minutes, until the edges are just starting to brown. Let the cookies cool on the baking sheet for 15 minutes and then transfer to a cooling rack to cool completely.

SMALL-BATCH CARROT CAKE COOKIES

As I shared on page 142, I think carrot cake is one of the greatest desserts of all time. And shockingly, I still stand by that statement, all these pages later! This small-batch recipe is ideal when the carrot cake craving hits but you're only baking for one or two. The result is two soft, moist cookies topped with the perfect amount of cream cheese frosting.

MAKES 2 EXTRA-LARGE COOKIES

Carrot Cake Cookies

⅓ cup (72 g) brown sugar
¼ cup (56 g) salted butter, melted
1 tablespoon plain Greek yogurt, room temperature
½ teaspoon vanilla extract
¾ cup (98 g) all-purpose flour
¼ teaspoon baking soda
¼ teaspoon ground cinnamon
¼ teaspoon Diamond Crystal kosher salt
¼ cup (30 g) grated carrots (see Note)

Cream Cheese Frosting

¼ cup (56 g) cream cheese, room temperature
1 tablespoon salted butter, room temperature
½ cup (56 g) powdered sugar, sifted
¼ teaspoon vanilla extract

NOTE
I like using finely grated carrots for these cookies. Use a microplane or the finest side of a box grater for the best results.

1. Preheat the oven to 350°F (180°C). Line a baking sheet with parchment paper.
2. Make the cookies: Place the brown sugar and butter in a medium bowl. Use a rubber spatula to mix until well combined, about 2 minutes.
3. Add the yogurt and vanilla extract and mix until combined, about 1 minute.
4. Add the flour, baking soda, cinnamon, and salt and mix until almost combined with only a few streaks of flour remaining, about 1 minute.
5. Add the carrots and mix until evenly distributed throughout the dough.
6. Use your hands to divide the dough in half and shape each half into a ball. Place both dough balls on the baking sheet, spaced equally apart.
7. Bake for 10 to 13 minutes, until the middles are just set. Let the cookies cool on the baking sheet for 10 minutes and then transfer to a cooling rack to cool completely.
8. Meanwhile, make the frosting: Place the cream cheese and butter in a medium bowl. Use a stand mixer or hand mixer to mix until well combined and smooth, about 2 minutes. Add the powdered sugar and vanilla extract and mix to form a smooth frosting, about 3 minutes.
9. When the cookies are completely cool, use a piping bag to pipe 2 to 3 tablespoons of frosting onto each cookie.

STUFFED COOKIES

In this chapter, "stuffed cookies" refers to two different stuffing methods. The first method involves sandwiching two cookies together with some sort of frosting or filling (like the Coconut Lime Cookies on page 229). The second involves stuffing frosting, chocolate, or another spread in the middle of each dough ball so that it bakes into the center of the cookie (like the Pistachio Cream Stuffed Cookies on page 244). All of these layered treats reveal an unexpected surprise in the center. They are deeply satisfying and perfect for when you want to impress someone or experiment with new combinations.

CINNAMON AND MILK CHOCOLATE COOKIES

WITH HAZELNUT CREAM FILLING

Cinnamon and milk chocolate is a bit of an unlikely combination, but it works really well, especially when combined with hazelnut cream. The sweetness of the milk chocolate brings out the warmth of the cinnamon, and the hazelnut cream provides a nuttiness that brings everything together. This is the type of cookie that looks and tastes very impressive but requires very little extra work compared to any regular old cookie. So, if you're in the market to impress anyone (yourself included), give these a go.

MAKES 9 LARGE COOKIES

9 tablespoons hazelnut cream (see Note)
¾ cup (170 g) salted butter
¾ cup (162 g) brown sugar
¼ cup plus 2 tablespoons (75 g) granulated sugar
1 large egg, room temperature
1 teaspoon vanilla extract
1½ cups (195 g) all-purpose flour
1 teaspoon ground cinnamon
1 teaspoon Diamond Crystal kosher salt
½ teaspoon baking powder
½ teaspoon baking soda
½ cup (85 g) milk chocolate chunks
Flaky salt, for topping

NOTE

Hazelnut cream is not Nutella. It's a sweetened hazelnut butter, similar to a pistachio cream. If you cannot find hazelnut cream, you can use pistachio cream instead.

1. Use a small (1-tablespoon/½-ounce) cookie scoop or measuring spoon to scoop the hazelnut cream into balls and place them on a plate lined with parchment paper. Transfer to the freezer to chill until hardened, about 15 minutes.
2. Heat a large pan over medium heat. Add the butter and stir as the butter melts, begins to bubble, and foams up, about 6 minutes. After the foam subsides, you'll see brown flecks at the bottom of the pan, and the butter will smell very nutty. Pour the brown butter into a large heat-safe bowl and transfer to the freezer to chill for about 10 minutes, until the butter is warm but no longer hot to the touch.
3. Add the brown sugar and granulated sugar to the bowl with the butter. Use a hand mixer or stand mixer to mix until well combined. Add the egg and vanilla extract and mix until combined.
4. Add the flour, cinnamon, kosher salt, baking powder, and baking soda. Mix on low until just combined, about 30 seconds.
5. Add the chocolate chunks and mix on low until evenly distributed throughout the dough.
6. Remove the chunks of hazelnut cream from the freezer. Use a large (4-tablespoon/2-ounce) cookie scoop to scoop the dough into balls. For each ball, with the dough still in the cookie scoop, use your fingers to make a 1-inch-deep (2.5 cm) indent in the dough. Add a chunk of hazelnut cream to the center and then close the dough around the cream, making sure it's completely sealed.

7. Place the dough in an airtight container and transfer to the fridge to chill for at least 4 hours, preferably overnight.
8. Preheat the oven to 350°F (180°C). Line two baking sheets with parchment paper.
9. Place up to five dough balls onto each baking sheet, spaced equally apart. Bake for 12 to 14 minutes, until the edges are starting to brown. Let the cookies cool on the baking sheets for 10 minutes and then transfer to a cooling rack to cool completely. Top each cookie with a pinch of flaky salt.

STRAWBERRY CHEESECAKE COOKIES

When I was young, I was a sucker for the no-bake JELL-O strawberry cheesecake mixes you could buy and make at home with a handful of ingredients. My eight-year-old self felt so empowered every time I whipped up one all by myself, plus I was obsessed with all things cheesecake—so I can only imagine how much that younger self would have loved these cookies. Freeze-dried strawberries and graham cracker chunks are added to the dough and then a thick hunk of cream cheese filling is stuffed inside each cookie. If you eat them warm, the filling is soft and gooey, and if you eat them cold, the filling sets up and tastes just like cheesecake. I prefer the latter, but dealer's choice.

MAKES 9 LARGE COOKIES

Cream Cheese Filling

4 ounces (113 g) cream cheese, softened

½ cup (56 g) powdered sugar

Strawberry and Graham Cracker Cookies

½ cup (113 g) salted butter, softened

2 tablespoons cream cheese, softened

⅔ cup (144 g) brown sugar

¼ cup (50 g) granulated sugar

1 large egg, room temperature

1 teaspoon vanilla extract

1½ cups (195 g) all-purpose flour

½ teaspoon baking soda

½ teaspoon Diamond Crystal kosher salt

5 or 6 graham cracker sheets, plus extra for topping

½ cup (10 g) freeze-dried strawberries, plus extra for topping

1. Make the filling: Place the cream cheese and powdered sugar in a medium bowl. Use a hand mixer or stand mixer to mix until smooth and creamy, about 2 minutes. Use a small (1-tablespoon/½-ounce) cookie scoop to scoop the filling onto a plate or small baking sheet lined with parchment paper. Transfer to the freezer to harden for at least 20 minutes.
2. Preheat the oven to 350°F (180°C). Line two baking sheets with parchment paper.
3. Make the cookies: Place the butter and cream cheese in a large bowl. Use a stand mixer or hand mixer to mix until fully combined, about 1 minute.
4. Add the brown sugar and granulated sugar and mix until fully combined, about 2 minutes.
5. Add the egg and vanilla extract and mix until fluffy and lighter in color, about 1 minute.
6. Add the flour, baking soda, and salt and mix on low just until the flour is combined.
7. Break the graham cracker sheets into ½-inch (1 cm) chunks and add to the dough. Add the freeze-dried strawberries (see Note). Mix on low until evenly distributed throughout the dough.
8. Remove the chunks of cream cheese filling from the freezer. Use a large (4-tablespoon/2-ounce) cookie scoop to scoop the dough into balls. For each ball, with the dough still in the cookie scoop, use your fingers to make a 1-inch-deep (2.5 cm) indent in the dough. Add a chunk of cream cheese filling to the center and then close the dough around the filling, making sure it's completely sealed.

9. Place up to five dough balls onto each baking sheet, spaced equally apart. Use the palm of your hand to slightly flatten each dough ball (so the ball is about 1 inch/2.5 cm tall) into more of a cylinder shape. Top each dough ball with a graham cracker chunk, gently pressing it into the dough.
10. Bake for 10 to 13 minutes, until the edges are just set. Gently press a freeze-dried strawberry into the top of each cookie. Let the cookies cool on the baking sheets for 10 minutes and then transfer to a cooling rack to cool completely. Store any extra cookies in the fridge.

NOTE

If the freeze-dried strawberries seem excessively large, break them into smaller pieces before adding to the dough.

COCONUT LIME COOKIES

When I was around nine years old, my family took a vacation to an all-inclusive resort in Mexico. There were approximately one hundred things to do around the resort, but I spent at least 90 percent of my time ordering virgin piña coladas. I was getting my parents' money's worth by drinking at least twenty of them a day, and I really wish I were exaggerating. For obvious reasons, I have such fond memories of that trip, and this cookie takes me back there every time. It includes lime instead of pineapple but still has such a fresh, tropical taste. It's also filled with a coconut buttercream that really sets it up for greatness. You too can take a bite of these and feel like you're in a lazy river sipping your twentieth tropical drink of the day.

MAKES 10 MEDIUM COOKIE SANDWICHES

Coconut Lime Cookies

¾ cup (150 g) granulated sugar

Zest of 3 limes (about 2 tablespoons)

½ cup (113 g) salted butter, softened

⅓ cup (72 g) brown sugar

1 large egg, room temperature

1 teaspoon vanilla extract

1⅓ cups (173 g) all-purpose flour

½ teaspoon baking powder

½ teaspoon Diamond Crystal kosher salt

¾ cup (45 g) unsweetened shredded coconut

Coconut Buttercream Frosting

1 cup (113 g) powdered sugar

¼ cup (56 g) salted butter, softened

1 tablespoon coconut milk

½ teaspoon vanilla extract

¼ cup (15 g) unsweetened shredded coconut

1. Preheat the oven to 350°F (180°C). Line two baking sheets with parchment paper.
2. Make the cookies: Place the granulated sugar and lime zest in a large bowl. Use your fingers to rub the lime zest into the sugar, releasing the lime oil. Transfer ¼ cup (50 g) lime sugar to a small bowl.
3. Add the butter and brown sugar to the large bowl. Use a stand or hand mixer to mix until well combined, about 2 minutes. Add the egg and vanilla extract and mix until smooth.
4. Add the flour, baking powder, and salt. Mix on low just until the flour is combined. Add the coconut and mix on low until evenly distributed.
5. Use a medium (2-tablespoon/1-ounce) cookie scoop to scoop the dough into balls. Roll each ball in the palms of your hands until smooth and then roll in the reserved lime sugar and roll to coat.
6. Place up to eight dough balls onto each baking sheet, spaced equally apart. Bake for 10 to 12 minutes, until the edges are just set. Let cool on the baking sheets for 10 minutes and then cool completely on a cooling rack. Repeat to bake the remaining dough.
7. Meanwhile, make the frosting: Place the powdered sugar and butter in a medium bowl. Use a stand mixer or hand mixer to mix until smooth, about 2 minutes. Add the coconut milk and vanilla extract and mix for 1 more minute. Add the coconut and mix until just combined.
8. Flip over half of the cooled cookies. Add about 2 tablespoons of frosting to each flipped-over cookie and spread it out evenly. Sandwich with the remaining cookies.

PB&J COOKIE SANDWICHES

I am terrible at choosing favorites, but this is easily one of my favorite cookies in the book: all of the childhood nostalgia of a PB&J sandwich packed into a cookie. Two soft peanut butter miso cookies are sandwiched with a smooth PB&J buttercream that you'll want to put on everything. The miso adds a slight salty-umami flavor to the cookies that perfectly complements the peanut butter and keeps it from being too peanut buttery (if that's even a thing). The nostalgia hits hard with these, and I truly cannot stop making them.

MAKES 6 LARGE COOKIE SANDWICHES

Peanut Butter Miso Cookies

¾ cup (162 g) brown sugar
½ cup (113 g) salted butter, softened
¼ cup (50 g) granulated sugar
½ cup (135 g) peanut butter
1 large egg plus 1 large egg yolk, room temperature
2 tablespoons white miso paste
1 teaspoon vanilla extract
1¼ cups (162 g) all-purpose flour
1 teaspoon baking soda
1 teaspoon ground cinnamon
½ teaspoon Diamond Crystal kosher salt

PB&J Buttercream

½ cup (135 g) peanut butter
½ cup (113 g) salted butter, softened
1½ cups (170 g) powdered sugar
1 teaspoon vanilla extract
Pinch of Diamond Crystal kosher salt
¼ cup (85 g) jam of choice

1. Preheat the oven to 350°F (180°C). Line two baking sheets with parchment paper.
2. Make the cookies: Place the brown sugar, butter, and granulated sugar in a large bowl. Use a stand mixer or hand mixer to mix until well combined, about 2 minutes.
3. Add the peanut butter, egg, egg yolk, miso paste, and vanilla extract. Mix until combined and fluffy, about 1 minute.
4. Add the flour, baking soda, cinnamon, and salt. Mix on low until just combined, about 30 seconds.
5. Use a large (4-tablespoon/2-ounce) cookie scoop to scoop the dough into balls. Use your hands to roll each one into a smooth ball. Place up to six dough balls onto each baking sheet, spaced equally apart.
6. Bake for 10 to 12 minutes, until the edges are just set. Let the cookies cool on the baking sheets for 10 minutes and then transfer to a cooling rack to cool completely.
7. Make the buttercream: Place the peanut butter and butter in a medium bowl. Use a stand mixer or hand mixer to mix until well combined, about 1 minute.
8. Add the powdered sugar, vanilla extract, and salt. Mix on low and then increase the speed to medium and mix until combined and smooth, about 2 minutes.
9. Add the jam and mix on low until just combined, about 30 seconds.
10. When the cookies are completely cool, flip half of them over. Pipe about 2 tablespoons of buttercream onto the flipped-over cookies. Sandwich with the remaining cookies. Store any extra cookie sandwiches in the fridge.

NUTELLA-STUFFED CCC

Growing up, I did not like Nutella, and I really don't know why. In fact, I didn't like anything hazelnut flavored. But around age nineteen, I came to my senses and fell in love with Nutella and all things hazelnut. (Fun fact: My favorite gelato flavor is now hazelnut.) And there are few better combinations than Nutella and cookies, especially CCC. For this recipe, each cookie is stuffed with a tablespoon of Nutella and baked just long enough that the edges are slightly crunchy while the middle is soft and gooey. Then, each cookie is topped with a generous pinch of flaky salt to balance out the rich chocolate overload. My child self wouldn't dream of eating this cookie, but my current self cannot get enough.

MAKES 7 LARGE COOKIES

7 tablespoons Nutella

½ cup (113 g) salted butter, softened

½ cup (108 g) brown sugar

¼ cup (50 g) granulated sugar

1 large egg, room temperature

1 teaspoon vanilla extract

1⅓ cups (173 g) all-purpose flour

½ teaspoon baking powder

½ teaspoon baking soda

½ teaspoon Diamond Crystal kosher salt

½ cup (85 g) semisweet or dark chocolate chips, plus extra for topping (see Note)

½ cup (70 g) unsalted hazelnuts, chopped

Flaky salt, for topping

NOTE

I highly recommend using semisweet or dark chocolate chips here. The Nutella stuffing already makes these cookies quite rich, and using milk chocolate would make them too rich (imo), but if that's your jam, then go for it!

1. Use a small (1-tablespoon/½-ounce) cookie scoop or measuring spoon to scoop the Nutella into balls and place them on a plate lined with parchment paper. Transfer to the freezer to chill until hardened, about 15 minutes.
2. Preheat the oven to 350°F (180°C). Line two baking sheets with parchment paper.
3. Place the butter, brown sugar, and granulated sugar in a large bowl. Use a stand mixer or hand mixer to mix until combined, about 2 minutes.
4. Add the egg and vanilla extract and mix until fully combined, about 1 minute.
5. Add the flour, baking powder, baking soda, and kosher salt. Mix on low until just combined, about 30 seconds.
6. Add the chocolate chips and hazelnuts and mix just until evenly distributed throughout the dough.
7. Remove the Nutella from the freezer. Use a large (4-tablespoon/2-ounce) cookie scoop to scoop the dough into balls. For each ball, with the dough still in the cookie scoop, use your fingers to make a 1-inch-deep (2.5 cm) indent in the dough. Add a ball of Nutella to the center and then close the dough around the Nutella, making sure it's completely sealed.
8. Place up to four dough balls onto each baking sheet, spaced equally apart. Bake for 11 to 14 minutes, until the edges are just set. Place a few extra chocolate chips on top of each cookie while it is still hot (to make it look extra pretty) and top with a pinch of flaky salt.

STUFFED PUMPKIN SNICKERDOODLES

Every year when the pumpkin spice girlies emerge, these cookies are on my mind. Pillowy soft snickerdoodles packed with pumpkin puree and pumpkin spice have me welcoming the colder weather every time. And as if these cookies couldn't get any better, we're stuffing each one with a chunk of chocolate that gets melty and gooey for the perfect bite. Not a fan of chocolate? Add whatever stuffing you want—speculoos spread, cream cheese frosting, and caramel are all delicious options!

MAKES 10 LARGE COOKIES

1 cup (215 g) brown sugar

½ cup (113 g) salted butter, softened

¼ cup (56 g) pumpkin puree, room temperature

1 large egg, room temperature

1 teaspoon sour cream, room temperature

1 teaspoon vanilla extract

2 cups (260 g) all-purpose flour

1 teaspoon pumpkin pie spice

½ teaspoon baking soda

½ teaspoon cream of tartar

½ teaspoon Diamond Crystal kosher salt

10 dark or milk chocolate chunks

2 tablespoons granulated sugar

1 teaspoon ground cinnamon

1. Place the brown sugar and butter in a large bowl. Use a stand mixer or hand mixer to mix until creamy, about 2 minutes.
2. Add the pumpkin puree, egg, sour cream, and vanilla extract. Mix until combined, about 1 minute.
3. Add the flour, pumpkin pie spice, baking soda, cream of tartar, and salt. Mix on low until just combined, about 1 minute.
4. Cover the bowl and transfer to the fridge to chill for 1 hour. After 40 minutes, preheat the oven to 350°F (180°C). Line two baking sheets with parchment paper.
5. Use a large (4-tablespoon/2-ounce) cookie scoop to scoop the dough into balls. For each ball, with the dough still in the cookie scoop, use your fingers to make a 1-inch-deep (2.5 cm) indent in the dough. Add a piece of chocolate to the center and then close the dough around the chocolate, making sure it's completely sealed.
6. Mix the granulated sugar and cinnamon in a small bowl. Drop each dough ball into the cinnamon sugar and roll to coat.
7. Place up to six dough balls onto each baking sheet, spaced equally apart. Bake for 10 to 12 minutes, until the edges are just starting to set. Let the cookies cool on the baking sheet for 10 minutes and then transfer to a cooling rack to cool completely (see Note).

NOTE

These cookies need to cool completely to fully set up. If you dig in early, the cookie will be too soft and fall apart. So, be patient! If you're in a hurry, you can put them in the fridge to speed up the process.

CINNAMON OATMEAL COOKIE ICE CREAM SANDWICHES

When I first made these cookies, I asked my husband, Connor, to rate them for me. He said that, out of all the cookies I had ever made, these were in his "top two—and not number two." And if that doesn't have you sold on these cookies, they have accumulated well over half a million page views on my website and millions of views on my social media since I first shared them in 2022. They are just really good cookies. And I feel like you can tell how good they are from the combination of mix-ins: oats, white chocolate, toffee, graham crackers, and lots of cinnamon. Honestly, what sounds better than that? The only thing that sounded better to me was taking two of these cookies and sandwiching them with a thick pad of vanilla ice cream in between. Adding vanilla ice cream may have changed my life. And I don't think the average person is consuming enough ice cream sandwiches. So, if you feel like you fall into that category, go ahead and start with these. Thank me later.

MAKES 11 MEDIUM COOKIE SANDWICHES

½ cup (113 g) salted butter, softened

½ cup (100 g) granulated sugar

¼ cup (54 g) brown sugar

1 large egg, room temperature

1 teaspoon vanilla extract

1 cup (130 g) all-purpose flour

¾ cup (68 g) rolled oats

1½ teaspoons ground cinnamon

½ teaspoon Diamond Crystal kosher salt

¼ teaspoon baking powder

¼ teaspoon baking soda

¼ cup (42 g) white chocolate chips

¼ cup (40 g) toffee bits

¼ cup (20 g) graham cracker chunks (1 to 2 sheets)

1 pint (473 ml) vanilla ice cream

1. Preheat the oven to 350°F (180°C). Line two baking sheets with parchment paper.
2. Place the butter, granulated sugar, and brown sugar in a large bowl. Use a stand mixer or hand mixer to mix until fully combined.
3. Add the egg and vanilla extract and mix until creamy, about 1 minute.
4. Add the flour, oats, cinnamon, salt, baking powder, and baking soda. Mix on low just until no streaks of flour remain, about 30 seconds.
5. Add the white chocolate chips, toffee, and graham cracker chunks. Mix on low until evenly distributed through the dough.
6. Use a medium (2-tablespoon/1-ounce) cookie scoop to scoop the dough into balls. Place up to eleven dough balls onto each baking sheet, spaced equally apart.
7. Bake for 9 to 11 minutes, until the edges are just starting to set. Let the cookies cool on the baking sheets for 10 minutes and then transfer to a cooling rack to cool completely.
8. Flip over half of the cookies. Add 2 to 3 tablespoons of vanilla ice cream onto the flipped cookies. Sandwich with the remaining cookies and enjoy immediately. Store any extra cookie sandwiches in the freezer.

LEMON COOKIE SANDWICHES

WITH LEMON CURD AND MASCARPONE FROSTING

You've probably had a lemon cookie before, but you've probably never had a lemon cookie quite like this. Soft lemon sugar cookies sandwich a smooth mascarpone frosting and a dollop of lemon curd. The mascarpone gives the frosting a slight tang, different from a cream cheese tang. It's what really ties these cookies together and will make them your new favorites.

MAKES 12 MEDIUM COOKIE SANDWICHES

Lemon Cookies

1¼ cups (250 g) granulated sugar

Zest of 2 lemons (about 2 tablespoons)

¾ cup (170 g) salted butter, softened

¼ cup (56 g) mascarpone, room temperature

1 large egg plus 1 large egg yolk, room temperature

1 teaspoon vanilla extract

2 cups (260 g) all-purpose flour

1 teaspoon Diamond Crystal kosher salt

½ teaspoon baking powder

½ teaspoon baking soda

Mascarpone Frosting

½ cup mascarpone (113 g), room temperature

3 tablespoons salted butter, room temperature

½ teaspoon vanilla extract

2 cups (227 g) powdered sugar

Pinch of Diamond Crystal kosher salt

Filling

2 tablespoons lemon curd

1. Preheat the oven to 350°F (180°C). Line two baking sheets with parchment paper.
2. Make the cookies: Place the sugar and lemon zest in a large bowl. Use your fingers to rub the lemon zest into the sugar, releasing the lemon oil.
3. Add the butter and use a stand mixer or hand mixer to mix until well combined, about 3 minutes.
4. Add the mascarpone, egg, egg yolk, and vanilla extract. Mix until well combined, about 2 minutes.
5. Add the flour, salt, baking powder, and baking soda. Mix on low until the flour is just combined, about 30 seconds.
6. Use a medium (2-tablespoon/1-ounce) cookie scoop to scoop the dough into balls. Place up to eight dough balls onto each baking sheet, spaced equally apart.
7. Bake for 8 to 10 minutes, until the edges are just set. Let the cookies cool on the baking sheets for 5 minutes and then transfer to a cooling rack to cool completely.
8. Repeat steps 6 and 7 to bake the remaining dough.
9. Meanwhile, make the frosting: Place the mascarpone, butter, and vanilla extract in a medium bowl. Use a stand mixer or hand mixer to mix until well combined, about 2 minutes. Add the powdered sugar and salt. Mix to form a smooth and creamy frosting, about 2 minutes. Transfer the frosting to a piping bag.

10. When the cookies are completely cool, flip half of the cookies over.
11. Pipe a circle of frosting on the flipped cookies, about ¼ inch (6 mm) from the edge. Add about ½ teaspoon lemon curd to the center of each circle.
12. Top each frosted cookie with an unfrosted one, gently pressing down to sandwich them together. Transfer to the fridge until ready to serve. Store any extra cookie sandwiches in the fridge.

STUFFED RED VELVET COOKIES

I was well into my teens when I realized that red velvet was actually just chocolate with some red food coloring added. I loved red velvet cake but didn't care for chocolate cake (I love chocolate cake now, don't worry), so you can bet that that revelation blew my mind. OK, OK, I know that is an oversimplification—red velvet has far less cocoa powder and no melted chocolate, so the chocolate flavor is much milder. It also often contains more of some sort of acid, giving it more of a tangy flavor (in traditional red velvet cakes, the red color comes from the acidic reaction between buttermilk and cocoa powder). Regardless, I'm still a big fan of red velvet in any form. These cookies are stuffed with a tangy cream cheese frosting and rolled in turbinado sugar for a satisfying crunch.

MAKES 7 LARGE COOKIES

Cream Cheese Frosting

4 ounces (113 g) cream cheese, softened

⅓ cup (38 g) powdered sugar

½ teaspoon vanilla extract

⅛ teaspoon Diamond Crystal kosher salt

Red Velvet Cookies

⅔ cup (133 g) granulated sugar

½ cup (113 g) salted butter, softened

1 large egg, room temperature

1 teaspoon vanilla extract

½ to 1 teaspoon red food coloring (see Note)

1¼ cups (162 g) all-purpose flour

2 tablespoons cocoa powder

½ teaspoon baking powder

½ teaspoon Diamond Crystal kosher salt

¼ cup (45 g) turbinado sugar

1. Make the frosting: Place the cream cheese, powdered sugar, vanilla extract, and salt in a medium bowl. Use a hand mixer or stand mixer to mix until smooth, about 2 minutes. Use a small (1-tablespoon/½-ounce) cookie scoop or measuring spoon to scoop the frosting into balls and place them on a small baking sheet or plate lined with parchment paper. Cover and transfer to the freezer to set up, about 15 minutes.
2. Preheat the oven to 350°F (180°C). Line two baking sheets with parchment paper.
3. Make the cookies: Place the sugar and butter in a large bowl. Use a stand mixer or hand mixer to mix until fully combined, about 2 minutes.
4. Add the egg, vanilla extract, and food coloring and mix until combined, about 1 minute.
5. Add the flour, cocoa powder, baking powder, and salt. Mix on low just until the flour is combined, about 30 seconds.
6. Remove the balls of cream cheese frosting from the freezer. Use a large (4-tablespoon/2-ounce) cookie scoop to scoop the dough into balls. For each ball, with the dough still in the cookie scoop, use your fingers to make a 1-inch-deep (2.5 cm) indent in the dough. Add a frosting ball to the center and then close the dough around the frosting, making sure it's completely sealed.
7. Place the turbinado sugar in a small shallow bowl. Roll each dough ball in the sugar to coat. Place up to four dough balls onto each baking sheet, spaced equally apart.

8. Bake for 12 to 15 minutes, until the edges are just set. Let the cookies cool on the baking sheets for 10 minutes and then transfer to a cooling rack to cool completely. Store any extra cookies in the fridge.

NOTE

Gel food coloring is brighter and more vibrant than liquid food coloring. If you're using gel food coloring, you'll need closer to ½ teaspoon, and if you're using liquid food coloring, use closer to 1 teaspoon.

RASPBERRY WHITE CHOCOLATE COOKIES

One of the first cookie recipes I ever developed was a raspberry white chocolate cookie. I was really proud of myself for this cookie, so much so that I wouldn't share the recipe with anyone for a long time. Then, I started my website, and I decided secret recipes are no fun—recipes are for everyone! This recipe is very similar to that cookie but with a few key changes and additions that make it even better. A brown sugar dough is mixed with freeze-dried raspberries (which provide such a perfect raspberry flavor without any extra moisture) and white chocolate chunks, and then each cookie is filled with raspberry jam. I love using a jam that is slightly tart to balance out the sweetness of the cookie.

MAKES 8 LARGE COOKIES

8 teaspoons raspberry jam (see Notes 1 and 2)

¾ cup (162 g) brown sugar

½ cup (113 g) salted butter, softened

1 large egg, room temperature

1 teaspoon vanilla extract

1¼ cups (162 g) all-purpose flour

1 tablespoon cornstarch

1 teaspoon Diamond Crystal kosher salt

½ teaspoon baking soda

½ cup (85 g) white chocolate chunks or chips

½ cup (10 g) freeze-dried raspberries (see Note 3)

1. Line a plate with parchment paper. Use a spoon to scoop 1-teaspoon dollops of raspberry jam onto the plate. Transfer to the freezer to harden for at least 15 minutes while you make the dough.
2. Preheat the oven to 350°F (180°C). Line two baking sheets with parchment paper.
3. Place the brown sugar and butter in a large bowl. Use a hand mixer or stand mixer to mix until well combined, about 3 minutes.
4. Add the egg and vanilla extract. Mix until fluffy and lighter in color, about 1 minute.
5. Add the flour, cornstarch, salt, and baking soda. Mix on low until just combined, about 30 seconds.
6. Mix in the chocolate chunks and raspberries on low until just combined.
7. Remove the jam from the freezer. Use a large (4-tablespoon/2-ounce) cookie scoop to scoop the dough into balls. For each ball, with the dough still in the cookie scoop, use your fingers to make a 1-inch-deep (2.5 cm) indent in the dough. Add a ball of jam to the center and then gently close the dough around the jam, making sure all of the jam is enclosed within the dough.
8. Place four dough balls onto each baking sheet, spaced equally apart. Bake for 9 to 12 minutes, until the edges are just starting to set.
9. Let the cookies cool on the baking sheets for 10 minutes and then transfer to a cooling rack to cool completely. Store any extra cookies in the fridge.

NOTES

1. If you don't want to stuff these cookies, that's fine! Just leave out the raspberry jam.

2. Tart raspberry jam is my favorite, but use whatever kind of jam you'd like.

3. If you can't find freeze-dried raspberries, use freeze-dried strawberries or blueberries instead. Fresh fruit will add too much liquid to these cookies.

PISTACHIO CREAM STUFFED COOKIES

As a kid, I hated all things pistachio flavored. I didn't mind the nuts themselves, but pistachios in cakes, cookies, and ice creams were a big no for me. Then I found myself in Rome, Italy, at the ripe age of twenty-two, and I tried pistachio gelato for the first time. I was healed on the spot and realized I'd had it all wrong. Pistachio shot to the top of my flavor list, and I've never looked back. Give me all the pistachio things, and I'll love you forever. Recently, I discovered pistachio cream—it's usually a nutty, creamy, and sweet mixture of pistachio butter and white chocolate. The first time I tried a spoonful, it nearly brought me to my knees, and I knew it had to be in a cookie. In this recipe, chunks of pistachio cream are stuffed inside a brown sugar dough studded with white chocolate chunks. If you hate all things pistachio, try these out, and they might be your pistachio gelato moment that will turn your whole life upside down.

MAKES 11 LARGE COOKIES

½ cup plus 3 tablespoons (165 g) pistachio cream

¾ cup (170 g) cold salted butter, divided

¾ cup (162 g) brown sugar

⅓ cup (66 g) granulated sugar

1 large egg plus 1 large egg yolk, room temperature

1 teaspoon vanilla extract

2 cups (260 g) all-purpose flour

1 teaspoon baking powder

1 teaspoon Diamond Crystal kosher salt

½ teaspoon baking soda

1 cup (170 g) white chocolate chunks

1. Use a small (1-tablespoon/½-ounce) cookie scoop or measuring spoon to scoop the pistachio cream into balls and place them on a plate lined with parchment paper. Transfer to the freezer to chill until hardened, at least 15 minutes.
2. Place 6 tablespoons (85 g) butter in a large bowl. Heat a medium pan over medium-low heat and add the remaining 6 tablespoons (85 g) butter. Stir as the butter melts, begins to bubble, and foams, about 5 minutes. After the foam subsides, you'll see brown flecks at the bottom of the pan, and the butter will smell very nutty. Pour the brown butter into the large bowl with the remaining butter. Stir while the hot brown butter melts the rest of the butter.
3. Add the brown sugar and granulated sugar to the large bowl. Use a stand mixer or hand mixer to mix until well combined.
4. Add the egg, egg yolk, and vanilla extract. Mix until combined and creamy, about 2 minutes.
5. Add the flour, baking powder, salt, and baking soda. Mix just until no streaks of flour remain.
6. Add the white chocolate chunks and mix on low until evenly distributed through the dough.
7. Remove the chunks of pistachio cream from the freezer. Use a large (4-tablespoon/2-ounce) cookie scoop to scoop the dough into balls. For each ball, with the dough still in the cookie scoop, use your fingers to make a 1-inch-deep (2.5 cm) indent in

the dough. Add a chunk of pistachio cream to the center and then close the dough around the cream, making sure it's completely sealed.

8. Place the dough in an airtight container and transfer to the fridge to chill for at least 8 hours or up to 48 hours.
9. Preheat the oven to 350°F (180°C). Line two baking sheets with parchment paper.
10. Place up to six dough balls onto each baking sheet, spaced equally apart.
11. Bake for 11 to 14 minutes, until the edges are just starting to set. Let the cookies cool on the baking sheets for 10 minutes and then transfer to a cooling rack to cool completely.

INDEX

D

E

F

G

H

I

J

K

L

M

R

S

T

U

V

W

Y

ACKNOWLEDGMENTS

To my online community. Without you making, loving, and sharing my cookie recipes for the past few years, we wouldn't be here today. I still get beyond excited every time I see a picture or video from your kitchen of you making my recipes.

To Connor, for loving me endlessly. You've supported me in my career since day one, long before I saw any success. You've cheered me on, mostly behind the scenes, and I wouldn't be where I am today without you. You tried every single cookie in this book and helped me tweak and fix each one. This book wouldn't exist without you!

To Emi, for loving cookie dough as much as I do. You tested all of these cookies at least once with me, and luckily, you loved every single one. I'm so proud of you for learning how to crack an egg all on your own and becoming a master of the stand mixer! You are my muse and my world.

To my mom and dad, for teaching me how to bake and cook as a little girl. I remember how excited I felt when you bought me my first cookbook, and just look at me now: your little girl with a cookbook of her own! Thank you for believing in me, always, even when I had the crazy idea to pursue a food blog out of your basement during a worldwide pandemic. And thank you for the hours and hours you watched Emi throughout this process so I could test cookies and write and test cookies some more.

To Brooke and Tom, for loving me since the day I met you and supporting me and Connor through every wild career decision we make. Thank you for the endless hours you watched Emi as well. I could not have done this without your help.

To my friend Brinley, for being a listening ear throughout this whole process. You talked me through several creative ruts I hit and helped me narrow in on my vision for several elements of this book.

To my manager, Charlotte Collie. You encouraged me to start this whole process. It was always a dream of mine to write a cookbook, and you helped me realize that I was capable enough and now was the right time.

To my editor, Olivia Peluso. Immediately after our first meeting, I knew you were the perfect editor for me. You made this process as smooth and enjoyable and easy as it could possibly be. (And to your partner, Robbie, for being such a team player and helping with last-minute details of the photoshoot.)

To my agent, Alison Fargis. You believed in the Cookie Club from day one. You helped me navigate the world of book publishing and advocated for everything I needed.

To my photographer, Nico Schinco. When initially selecting a photographer, I was drawn to the way you worked with light. Then I was more amazed to watch your process in real life. Your vision for this project blew me away, and your warm and genuine personality made our photoshoot such a wonderful experience.

To my food stylist, Katie Wayne. I was in awe of how effortlessly you moved through the kitchen. You handled my recipes beautifully, and I was so impressed by your ideas for each photo. And I was so honored when you reacted with a "wow" every time you tried each of the cookies in this book.

To my food stylist assistant, Nikki Jessop. You are so graceful and intentional in the kitchen. I appreciated how often you asked me for input and clarification to make sure every cookie turned out perfect.

To my prop stylist, Ashleigh Sarbone. The props you pulled for this shoot constantly impressed me. I am so glad you were on this team.

To my publicist, Delaney Vetter. You were on board with this concept from the minute you heard about it. Your creativity and excitement transformed this project.

To my illustrator, Giovana Cavalcante, thank you for taking on this project. I have been obsessed with your work for a long time and was so thrilled you were so willing and excited to be part of this. Your work is so special and truly brought this book to life.

To my art director, William Thomas. Thank you for your patience. It took me insanely long to decide what I wanted this book to look like, and even after that, I changed my mind a million times. Thank you for making this book exactly what I wanted it to be.

To my official recipe testers, Greg and Ben. Your meticulous notes and feedback helped me refine and reshape these cookies into the best they could be.

To my community of recipe testers. I read through every piece of feedback each of you sent. Your notes and thoughts on each cookie were beyond useful and helped shape this book into what it is.

ABOUT THE AUTHOR

Mallory Oniki is the recipe developer and creator behind The Palatable Life. She is best known on social media for her unique and inventive cookie recipes, but she also shares a wide variety of sweet and savory recipes for home cooks. Her work has been featured on *The Rachael Ray Show* and *Good Morning America* and in *Taste of Home* and Food52, among others. She lives with her husband, Connor, and daughter, Emi.